WITNESS TO EVIL

My Father's Murder. My Mother's Guilt.
My Struggle for Justice in a House of Tyranny.

VERONICA MCGRATH

HACHETTE
BOOKS
IRELAND

Copyright © 2011 Veronica McGrath
First published in 2011 by Hachette Books Ireland
A Hachette UK Company

1

The right of Veronica McGrath to be identified as the Author of the Work has been asserted by her in accordance with the Copyright, Designs and Patents Act, 1988.

Written with Yvonne Kinsella and June Considine

A CIP catalogue record for this title is available from the British Library.

ISBN 978 1 4447 2444 8

Typeset in Sabon by Hachette Books Ireland
Cover design by ampvisual.com
Printed and bound in Great Britain by Mackays, Chatham ME5 8TD

Hachette Books Ireland policy is to use papers that are natural, renewable and recyclable products and made from wood grown in sustainable forests. The logging and manufacturing processes are expected to conform to the environmental regulations of the country of origin.

Hachette Books Ireland
8 Castlecourt Centre
Castleknock
Dublin 15
Ireland

www.hachette.ie

A division of Hachette UK
338 Euston Road, London NW1 3BH
England

This book is dedicated to the memory of my loving father, Brian (Bernard) McGrath. I hope that you can now finally rest in peace, Dad. I will love you and miss you for the rest of my life.

Some of the names and some details of individuals have been changed in the book in order to protect their privacy.

CONTENTS

'What lies behind us and what lies before us are tiny matters compared to what lies within us.'

A saying given to me by a lady from the Woman's Trust organisation in the UK

Foreword

By retired Detective Garda John Maunsell, the first investigating officer on the case.

I remember the case of Bernard McGrath very well because it was one that was not solved until after my retirement, and I always regretted never being able to see justice done during my time as a member of the Garda Síochána.

My involvement started back in 1993, when I was contacted by a solicitor who told me of an alleged unsolved murder. At the time I was stationed in Tallaght Garda Station in south Dublin and I was informed that a partner of Veronica's had gone to this solicitor and told him what Veronica had alleged happened to her father on the land where they lived in Coole, County Westmeath six years earlier. Her

11

partner was shocked by what he had heard and he felt that he had to do something.

The solicitor phoned me after listening to the story and told me that he found the events very hard to believe, but he had to have it checked out. I have to admit, I found it hard to believe myself, but the next day myself and another Detective Garda, Kevin Tunney, drove up to Navan, where Veronica McGrath was living at the time, to talk to her.

Veronica was happy, but nervous, to see us and she related the story to us in detail. We immediately contacted the Superintendent from Granard in Longford, and Veronica told him exactly the same story. We went back to Navan a day or two later and took a full statement from her. Each time the story was the same and it was clear to us from day one that Veronica was an innocent party in this murder.

Having taken a number of statements from Veronica, the Garda Technical Bureau from Garda Headquarters in Dublin and the local detectives from Granard subsequently carried out a dig of the land where the body was allegedly buried. Through this, they discovered fragments of bone and teeth.

But while they were able to prove that the remains were in fact human, they couldn't say for certain that they were those of Bernard McGrath.

Back then, DNA testing was in its infancy and investigating officers believed that, in order to ensure that the case stood up in court, they would have needed to carry out DNA tests to confirm that the bones and teeth found were in fact those of Bernard McGrath.

At this stage there was no way of proving that Mr McGrath was even dead, except for the statement given by Veronica. But I always knew that Veronica was telling the truth and although she helped clean up the blood stains the next morning I knew that she was under immense duress and that she was terrified not to do what her mother had ordered her to do.

She appeared to me at the time to be a very vulnerable young woman who was genuinely afraid of her mother and what she may have done had she gone to the Gardaí and reported what had happened.

At this stage Vera McGrath was living in Navan with a partner. She was visited by the Gardaí and at first denied the murder had ever taken place. She was taken in for questioning to the local Garda station. Then, while in the station, she actually admitted her part in the killing to a female Garda as she was being taken off to use the toilet.

As Vera McGrath was being interrogated, the Gardaí contacted the police in the UK and Colin Pinder was taken in for questioning where he almost immediately admitted his part in the killing. He gave police officers a story that suggested he helped kill Mr McGrath because he had been racially abused by him. He said at the time that he was very sorry for what had happened that night.

But despite this admittance of guilt on both sides of

the water, there was still no way of proving that the remains found were those of Bernard McGrath, or Brian as he was also known. And so, due to this lack of evidence, the case was eventually dropped in 1996.

However, when a person disappears the case is always left open, just in case a development arises in latter years, and this was the case with the disappearance of Bernard McGrath.

In 2007, while talking to a member of the Garda Cold Case Unit, who investigate unsolved murders, I told him about this case and I asked him would the unit take a look at it again.

I had retired in 2001 and it was one case that I always regretted not being able to solve – it always irked me. I knew that Bernard McGrath was dead and that he had been buried on that land.

But since the initial investigation in the 1990s, there had been huge developments in DNA testing, which meant that when the Cold Case Unit moved in to start an investigation, Gardaí were finally able to arrest and charge both Colin Pinder and Vera McGrath.

I was in court on and off during the trial as I was called to give evidence and I honestly do not think that Vera McGrath ever showed any sign of remorse over what she had done.

Pinder pleaded guilty from day one to manslaughter, but Vera McGrath never made a plea, despite her admittance years before.

I was unsure of how things would go right up until

the day the verdict was read out. Juries can be very fickle and I was concerned that they may have both walked free. But I have to say, I was very satisfied when the verdict was eventually read out.

I felt that Veronica was very harshly treated at times in court and I didn't think she deserved to be treated in this way. And I was aware that she'd had a hard life in the years following the murder.

At one stage during the trial the judge actually told the jury to treat Veronica as an accomplice, which I thought was very unfair. Not once did we, the Gardaí, believe Veronica had anything to do with the murder.

Yes, she helped clean up the mess the next day but we all knew that she was just terrified of what would have happened had she refused to help and that she had nothing to do with what happened that night in Coole.

I just hope that she can now finally move on with her life and rear her family in peace. She deserves that.

Detective John Maunsell, 2011

The Brian (Bernard) McGrath murder investigation was the first major murder trial for the Garda Serious Crime Review Team. It was seen as a huge success.

Could You Just Listen?

(A poem given to me by a friend, but for me the words say it all.)

When I ask you to listen to me
And you start giving me advice
You have not done what I have asked

When I ask you to listen to me
And you begin to tell me why I
shouldn't feel that way
You are trampling on my feelings

When I ask you to listen to me
And you feel you have to do something
to solve my problem
You have failed me; strange as it may
seem

Listen

All I asked was that you listen
Not talk or do
Just hear me through

I can do for myself
I am not helpless
Maybe discouraged and faltering
But not helpless

When you do something for me
That I can and need to do for myself
You contribute to my fear and
inadequacy

But when you accept as a simple fact
That I do feel, what I feel
No matter how irrational

Then I can quit trying to convince you
And get about the business of
understanding what's behind this
irrational feeling

When that's clear, the answers are
obvious and I don't need advice
Irrational feelings make more sense
When we understand what's behind
them

So please listen and just hear me

Anonymous

Prologue

My life was turned upside down on a night in 1987, some time between 10 March and 18 April. I wish I could recall the exact date and time that it happened. I wish I could remember every little detail, but I can't. And I doubt I ever will.

But what I do recall will stay with me for ever. That was the night when, aged eighteen, I looked on in horror as my mother and my fiancé brutally killed my father outside our home in a quiet rural townland. It was six long years before I alerted the authorities to what had taken place. During that time, I lived each day in fear of my mother, and of what would happen if I revealed her secret. I became a shadow of my former self. My mental health suffered so badly that the consequences would play out for decades to come.

Memories of that horrific night come back to me in

flashes. Sindy, our dog, barking frantically. My mother handing something to Colin Pinder, my fiancé. My father trying to protect himself behind a ladder, falling to the ground. Colin Pinder, the man I love and am soon to marry, and my mother, towering above me. The deadly looks on the faces.. Me rocking back and forth on the front steps of our house, saying, 'Oh, God, oh, God,' over and over. Feeling as though I'm disappearing, as everything around me becomes massive: the trees and bushes, the stars above. Noise, screaming. My eyes closing to the mayhem as I float up outside my body. I feel as though I have become tiny.

I run to my father, now hiding in a ditch, and hold him in my arms. 'Stay with me, Dad,' I say. 'I'll keep you safe.' But I can't. I don't. And then it's too late.

Some months later, I walk across a field towards a blazing fire. The putrid smell is in my nostrils. It hangs in the air. It is my dead father's funeral pyre. A round glowing object rolls from the fire on to the ground. It burns bright orange. Colin Pinder attempts to lift it into the fire with a pitchfork. This unthinkable image stays with me. It will torment my dreams for years to come. Twenty-three years later, the image of my father's burning, decapitated head has not gone away.

My father died savagely at the hands of people he believed he could trust. I was unable to prevent it happening. Since that day, my life has been haunted by one consuming question: why couldn't I save him? Why was I so powerless to prevent the brutal killing of the man I had adored throughout my childhood. It is not a question I can easily answer. To even begin to understand it is to journey into the darkest corners of my life. It is hard for me to go there, but I know I have to. It is in these places that all my ills – and there have been many – find their root.

The night my father was murdered marked the tragic end of my parents' tragic marriage. I became a victim of the events of that night. But I am no longer the cowed, controlled young woman I was then, living in fear of a tyrannical mother, brainwashed into believing I was stupid, ugly, insignificant. I am no longer tiny. I have come a long way, even if I usually took the hardest possible route.

I write this book in part to lay my own ghosts to rest. And, although nothing can bring back my beloved dad, by telling his story, I seek to honour the memory of a good man, and lay his ghost finally to rest, too.

The day I finally broke my vow of silence and confided everything I remembered of the night of my father's murder to the police was the second most frightening day of my life. But I did it. This is my story.

One

A Troubled Childhood

Brian McGrath's entrance into the world was not a happy one. On 20 August 1944, soon after his mother had given birth to him, he was wrapped in a blanket and deposited on the steps of the Catholic church in Castleblaney, County Monaghan. In those days it was not uncommon for a young unmarried woman to conceal her pregnancy and give birth alone and in secret. I often wonder how his poor mother must have felt when she left her son behind, knowing she would never hold him again. I can only imagine her grief and sense of helplessness.

According to my father, a local man who was walking his horse past the church came upon the little bundle. He handed over the newborn baby boy to the local nuns.

For the first years of his life, my father was reared in a convent in Drogheda. He was christened Brian (although some people called him Bernard). When he grew older he was sent to the Artane Industrial School on the northside of Dublin City. Occasionally he would speak to me about those years. He described Artane as an institution where only the strongest survived. If he 'misbehaved', the Christian Brothers would make him stand in a corner for hours on end. He described how some of the boys were regularly beaten, and I'm sure he, too, had his share of physical abuse. But mainly he told us it was a hard time in his life and left it at that.

On his sixteenth birthday, he left Artane. His parting gift from the Christian Brothers was an extra pair of boots to keep him going. He walked into Dublin City that day and was so scared of the world out there that he walked all the way back to Artane that evening. He asked the Christian Brothers if he could stay for just one more night and was surprised when they agreed. But he knew he had to strike out on his own. His time in Artane was over and he now had to fend for himself.

Shortly afterwards he met Vera on a beach in Portmarnock, County Dublin. He was still only sixteen and she was around four years younger. They got on well, and though they didn't form a relationship at that stage, they kept in touch. Dad went on to serve in the British Army for a few years and in that time they wrote letters to each other. Recently I found some of them. From what I read they were in love, and when he came back to Ireland they began to go out together.

When my mother was eighteen, they took the ship to England and were married in London, no family, no friends. My mother once told me that they had eloped to escape her family's disapproval of the marriage. Her parents were worried that she was too young to marry, and possibly also that my father, with his background in Artane and with no family to his name, was not good enough for her. On 13 May 1967, early in the morning, their wedding took place in the Church of the Most Sacred Heart of Jesus, in Eden Grove, Islington. Afterwards, the newlyweds went to a burger bar to celebrate. On their marriage certificate it states that my father was a bachelor and a gas fitter, and my mother was a spinster and an invoice typist. It gave my grandfather's name as John Langan; he was a dock worker. Sadly, a line had been struck through the section where my father's parents' names should have been. I'm sure this must have affected him. It certainly affected me when I first saw it.

My mother was working in a tobacco factory when she became pregnant with me. I was born in the Royal Free Hospital in north London on 4 August 1968 and was about two years old when my parents returned to Ireland. Initially, we stayed with my grandparents who lived in Finglas on the northside of Dublin. My granny was Frances Margaret, or 'Fanny', as my grandad, a warm, caring man, affectionately called her. She was a lovely woman, very dainty and attractive. She didn't drink or smoke, and her clothes were always smart and fashionable. She used to say to us, 'I'm the lady of Finglas,' and that was how I always saw her. Every day she walked to Superquinn, the local supermarket, with her trolley to do her shopping, and attended daily mass. My mother had two sisters and a brother, who always showed me the same affection. Throughout my childhood, my grandparents were a strong, stable presence in my life and I loved them to bits. They went everywhere together and would hold hands walking down the street. Sadly Grandad died when he was only sixty-three years old.

Soon enough, my father bought a small house off the North Strand Road in Dublin. It was on a corner and one door opened out on to Spencer Place, the other on to Northbrook Avenue. We had very little money but my father made it as comfortable as he could for us. He was handy around the house, always doing bits and pieces to give it a more homely feeling.

I was an only child until I was seven, when my brother Brian was born. If being an only child usually means receiving lots of attention from your parents, that wasn't my experience with my mother. I have no memories from my young life of being hugged or kissed by her, unless other people were present. At night, when I was going to bed and my father asked me to give her a goodnight kiss, she'd turn her face to the side, scrunch up her nose and mouth, and coldly offer me her cheek. I felt as though my very presence annoyed her, but I didn't understand why. Sometimes she would take to her bed for days on end and, though I didn't know what was wrong with her, I knew I should make my presence felt as little as possible. I'd feed myself with bread and jam and try not to make a noise or disturb her. I remember the relief when Dad would finally arrive home from work.

My strongest memory of those early years is of my unrelenting fear of displeasing my mother, of drawing her anger down on me. I can still remember the day she handed me a bar of Lifebuoy soap and told me that from now on I was responsible for washing my underwear. I was seven. Strangely enough, she discouraged me from looking after my teeth. She had dentures and I don't know if that was the reason she literally always pushed me out of the bathroom if she saw me with a toothbrush. I accepted this kind of behaviour as normal, and it was only after Brian came along that I began to see a different side to my mother. To him, she displayed love and affection. But if she could love him, why not me? From early on, it was impressed on me that I was to blame for this. I was not lovable.

On one occasion, when Brian was still a baby, I was told to mind him outside. I was playing in the street with my friends and sat him on a deep window ledge to watch us. At some stage during the game he toppled to the ground. He was bruised and shaken but he'd recovered by the time I brought him home. Too terrified to tell my mother the truth, I said he'd tripped on the path. Later, my friends called to see how he was. Not knowing what I'd told my mother, they described how he'd fallen. As soon as they left, my mother grabbed me by the hair and flung me across the kitchen. I've never forgotten the beating she gave me. But worse than that was the silence that followed. I don't know exactly how long it went on, but it felt like an eternity before life returned to normal in our house.

Within a few months of Brian's birth, my mother was pregnant again. After Andrew, my second brother, was born, it was my job to take the babies out for a walk. They both sat in a high pram, one at each end, and I'd walk around the streets for hours. The weather didn't matter. Hail, rain or shine, I stayed out as long as I could – I was punished if I came back too soon.

But my childhood is not all bleak memories. I recall the love I received from my grandparents, my aunts and my uncle, happy trips to the seaside in Howth and Dollymount with my grandparents or my father. I'd play for hours in the sand and sea, and fish for pinkeens. My mother's eldest sister used to buy clothes for me. Like my grandmother, she had an eye for fashion, and the things she chose were always perfect for me. I walked all over Dublin City with my father. He'd bring me to places of historical interest and tell me stories about the Viking raiders. We visited the

GPO where the Easter Rising took place and he explained how Ireland had become a republic. On Saturday night he'd polish my shoes and bring me to mass on Sunday. I always looked forward to Sundays because we'd meet all of our neighbours. And Dad seemed to know everyone.

Whatever love my parents shared when they were first married faded as the years passed. I thought their constant rows were a normal part of married life. Hearing their raised voices, I would try to make myself invisible, but it was impossible to stop the tension seeping into me. My dad seemed to draw my mother's wrath at the slightest thing. I always felt sorry for him and, in a way, her anger drew us even closer together.

I first became aware that my life was different from that of most other families on our road when I became friendly with two girls, Clara and Sally. Their parents were warm-hearted, open people and I was always welcome in their house. One day, when the girls were out walking with their mother, Sally tripped on the path and fell. She became very ill after she returned home. Her parents, thinking she was concussed from her fall, brought her to the hospital. It turned out that she had cancer. We were all devastated when we heard the shocking news. A simple fall on the street and the tests that followed had alerted the doctors to her condition. All I knew about cancer back then was that it was a very bad disease that killed people. It was a worrying time.

Sally received chemotherapy and lost all of her hair but I refused to believe she would die. I remember her asking for a Little Red Devil ice pop, her favourite, when she was nearing the final stages of her illness. Her mother told her that when she got to Heaven, Little Red Devil ice pops would be hanging from the branches of a tree that had been grown especially for her. It was heartbreaking to see the sorrow on the faces of her parents and her sister when she passed away.

Despite their grief, I remember feeling that they were a proper family. Sally's mother behaved like a real mother. It seemed so unfair that she had lost her little girl when she had always shown her children that she loved and cherished them. My mother had me, but was only capable of showing me contempt or indifference. Through this sad event, I began to see the reality of my relationship with her. But I still craved her love.

Soon after, my father sold our North Strand house and bought a bigger one in East Wall, facing Fairview Park. My father dabbled in everything – building, plumbing and odd jobs for people. When he worked as chauffeur and gardener for a well-known Dublin businessman he'd take us out for a spin in the expensive car. I felt grand and rich as we drove around the city. My mother was unhappy with the unsocial hours he had to work, a cause for more arguments, so he gave up his job and found other work. Shortly afterwards, he was made redundant and ended up on social welfare.

At that time my mother was working in the

Clontarf Castle, a hotel not too far from home. Dad remained determined to pay off his mortgage and most of his social welfare went on that. They were tough times. He could have handed the keys of our home back to the bank and walked away. I believe it was pride that stopped him. He always said that the last thing he wanted was to live in a council estate. He wasn't a snob, he had no airs or graces – and, indeed, we had far less than many people living in council estates back then. I believe his need to own a house stemmed from growing up with no home or family: he wanted to have somewhere he could finally call his.

One day the Electricity Supply Board came in and cut us off. My father was in despair. At night we used candles for light. I remember collecting wood from Fairview Park with him on many occasions. On cold nights we'd go up to a coal yard at the back of our house and climb the wall. We'd rob as much coal as we could carry, just the two of us. It's embarrassing, looking back on it, but that's what it was like in those days. Dad was determined to keep the house warm for his family and was prepared to pay the price if he got caught.

We also scoured the streets for empty mineral bottles; at that time you got sixpence for every one you returned. That money often put food on our table. At other times, when there was no money, we got by on slices of bread and tins of Campbell's soup. I remember going with Dad to the St Vincent de Paul charity headquarters. To me it looked like a huge house filled with shoes and clothes that we could take away with us. The Vincent de Paul was a great help to my family during those awful times.

One night I left the shoes I'd received from them beside the fire before I went to bed. When I got up the next morning they'd disappeared into thin air. Brian was about two at the time and a little livewire. It turned out he'd thrown my shoes into the fire and they'd burned to nothing. I was devastated when my mother made me walk to school that day in her high heels. I was only nine, and I don't know how I actually walked in them. They were way too big for me too, but it was that or walk in my bare feet.

Christmas was Dad's favourite time of the year. When he had money to spare, he loved to buy presents for everyone. My mother didn't believe in Christmas, or in birthday parties or Hallowe'en. Years later, when I was buying presents for my own children, she told me Christmas was a just a money-making racket and that I should know better than to be part of it. But my father always made sure we had a Christmas tree and decorations, and at least one present when we woke up on Christmas Day.

One particular Christmas when we were totally broke, a miracle happened. We were out together when Dad found an envelope in the middle of the road. He opened it and discovered a wad of money inside. It could have been somebody's wage packet but there was no name and no address on the envelope. He knew he'd never find out who owned the money – what else could he do but spend it? It was a week or so before Christmas and he bought me a Tiny Tears doll. That doll was on top of every little girl's Santy list that year. He bought presents for the boys, too, and we actually had money for a real feast. It was a fantastic Christmas, the best ever.

My two brothers were too young to go to school when we lived in Dublin but, initially, I went to the convent on North William Street. Later I was moved to a Protestant school nearer to our house, even though I was a Catholic. But my attendance at school was poor. And it wasn't all my mother's fault: I was self-conscious and shy, convinced I was the poorest child in the class. I didn't have a proper schoolbag, just a plastic one from a supermarket, and I thought everyone was laughing at me behind my back. Missing school was a relief and, with the housework and child-minding at home, I felt as if I had some purpose there – and doing something I was good at.

After my third brother Edward was born, my father made a decision that he'd long dreamed of, and our lives in Dublin soon drew to a close.

Two

Moving to the Countryside

Andrew, my second brother, suffered badly from eczema and asthma. My father, who had always wanted to live in the country, believed that the cleaner air would ease his conditions. I was about ten years old at the time and I remember his excitement every evening as he scoured the *Evening Press* property pages for houses outside Dublin. One evening he saw what he wanted. It was a small house for sale in a place called Coole, in County Westmeath, priced at £5,700.

He was delighted when he went to view it, even though it needed a lot of work, and he decided to buy it. Nearly every weekend we'd drive down to Coole where he'd do the necessary building and repairs. Dad was a real grafter and would put in long hours to get a job done. He drove a small Fiat back then, a Bambino.

Although it's unusual to see these cars on the road nowadays, every time I spot one I think of those weekends and how Dad was determined to make that house perfect for his family. I think he especially wanted to please my mother.

The house is the first one at the beginning of a side road and there is an acre of land around it. This pleased Dad no end. We referred to this field as 'the garden'. He was green-fingered and planned to plant potato beds and rows of vegetables. The countryside surrounding Coole is beautiful, and I was also looking forward to beginning a new life there.

When I started school I found it hard to settle in. I'd always had problems with spelling, writing and reading. If I recognised a word on the page and got it right, I might not recognise it the next time I came across it. Reading out loud was torture. I'd read the words the wrong way around and I'd get tired trying to figure out how to pronounce them. My writing wasn't a whole lot better so, inevitably, I thought of myself as stupid.

My dad had had very little education. His spelling was bad and my mother seemed to enjoy showing him up in front of visitors. She would ask him to spell words like 'sandwiches' or 'fridge', knowing he would become flustered and confused. Sometimes, she turned her attention to me. This usually happened during my homework when I had my list of words to spell. One word I always misspelled was 'apple' and then she would make me stand against the wall and repeat 'I am stupid' over and over. Other times it was 'I am fat' or 'I am ugly'. She tested my spelling in front of my friends. I found many words impossible and would end up mortified, convinced my friends agreed with her opinion that I was stupid.

I remember one time there was an outbreak of nits in the class, and I got them. My mother treated my hair with special shampoo, then got the scissors and began to hack away at it. I watched in horror as it fell to the floor in clumps and was afraid to look in the mirror for ages afterwards. When I finally did, I looked as awful as I'd feared: my hair stuck up at all angles. I was like an urchin from a strip cartoon. I'll never forget the shame of going to school with my new haircut.

I was also conscious of my Dublin accent and got teased a fair bit by some of my classmates for being a 'Jackeen'. My mother often gave me toast for my lunch. One particular pupil thought this was hilarious and used to jeer at me when I unwrapped my lunch. He'd tell me to put the toast on the radiator to keep it warm. One day I decided I'd had enough. I hit him and he struck me back. Before I knew what was happening, it had turned into a proper brawl and I definitely came off the worst. Incidents like that didn't help my confidence and I found it even more difficult to keep up in class. But I did make some friends in school and began to enjoy living in a small, quiet community.

Our house was old and there was always something

going wrong with it. I live there now and I can appreciate how hard it must have been for Dad to keep everything going. My mother never seemed to give him a moment's peace, and the tension between them got worse. He managed to hold it all together, despite the rows.

My mother was a very complicated woman, incredibly headstrong and controlling, and he found it hard to cope with her. The continuing arguments made me jittery – and they'd start at the drop of a hat. Everything would be calm in the house until one of them made a remark. Suddenly it was like a volcano erupting, all screaming and shouting, recrimination and anger. I didn't understand a lot of what was going on, how the rows seemed to explode from nothing. I've no doubt there was a pattern, and that both parents were locked into their own personal grievances. But all I knew as a kid was the fear I felt when it'd kick off. Outwardly, I'd never dare express my opinion. On the inside, though, I always sided with my dad. Perhaps my mother sensed how I felt. Perhaps it was the reason that I was the constant butt of her annoyance, why she always sought to undermine me, calling me ugly, stupid, or worse.

My father was so proud to have his own land, and loved the fresh country air. He would tend his vegetable garden and would be amazed at how he could walk for miles and hardly see a soul. He loved his walks. Manners were important to him. He reared us to be polite to people, to say 'please' and 'thank you' and to show respect for others. An old woman in her eighties who lives up the road from me still talks about how respectful he always was to her. He'd knock on her hall door, then lean his arms on her garden wall so that he didn't look as though he was pushing his way into her home. He'd help her with odd jobs but never accept a penny for it. He liked helping people and he's remembered locally as a gentleman who was always willing to oblige the community.

My mother's disappearances into the bedroom for long periods continued, and my job as carer grew more demanding now that there were three boys to look after. It was a role I took on gladly, so great was my need to please her and try to keep the uneasy peace. I would jump to her commands, always anxious to avoid a slap or one of her icy silences.

As I grew older, the sound of her footsteps coming from the bedroom into the kitchen told me all I needed to know about her mood. A heavy tread meant trouble. I'd start rushing around the kitchen, checking that there was nothing out of place, that her cigarettes were on the table, the kettle was on. Maybe a cup of tea would help. Not likely. I became expert on thinking up compliments to please her, comparing her to film stars, telling her she looked lovely, as indeed she did.

Her appearance meant everything to her. She was very pretty when she smiled: slim, young-looking, blonde. I felt like a dowdy shadow beside her, never more so than as I approached my teens, feeling spotty and having mood swings. My body was changing, but I was very innocent as to what was happening to me. I didn't know the first thing about the facts of life. When my first period came, I was still in primary school and got the shock of my life when I noticed the blood. I was in the school toilet at the time and I thought I was going to die. When I made my way back to the classroom, I was too scared to tell the teacher. I imagined being rushed to hospital, doctors examining me and operations being performed in that most private part of me. At break-time I confided in my best friend. I could tell from her face that, whatever it was, it was no big deal. She explained that this would happen to me once a month. It was part of growing up and becoming a woman. I would need sanitary towels and should ask my mother to buy them for me.

When I arrived home, I was doubled up with stomach cramps. I asked my mother why this was happening. She said nothing, left the room and came back with a wad of toilet paper, which she handed me. 'Put that in your knickers,' she said, and left the room again. That was the last we spoke of it.

A short while later, a friend of hers took me to one side and told me what was happening to my body and why. My mother must have asked her to do it. I couldn't understand why she wouldn't tell me herself and, deep down, I felt a sense of loss. Despite everything, I still longed to know that she cared – and this would have been her chance to show me. But she chose to leave me to my own devices. She never bought me sanitary towels. I had no money of my own and had to make do with toilet paper each month and pray that there would be enough in the house to get me through the week.

I started secondary school in Granard, and the problems I'd had with the three Rs really came to the fore. The classes were large and it was impossible to keep up with the curriculum. I found subjects like geography and history really hard and quickly began to slip behind. After a year I moved to the vocational school in Castlepollard where I fared a bit better. My father used to drive me there in the mornings. On the journey to school he'd occasionally stop and give people a lift on their way to work. He was so nervous of my mother's overreaction that, if the person was female, he'd ask me not to mention it in the house, in case my mother started screaming accusations at him. She was jealous, always quick to accuse him of flirting with other women.

I attended the vocational school in Castlepollard for two years and sat my Group Certificate. Happily I passed the exam. I also taught myself the basic chords on guitar. In those days, when it came to working with my hands – art, home economics, music – I was more confident. But I only had to open a book and I'd feel inadequate. Years later, in my early thirties, I would discover that I was dyslexic – but in those days I wouldn't have understood what the word meant or how significant it was in terms of my education. This was suggested by a London psychologist, who passed me on to a specialist in that field. I was then officially diagnosed. When I received this information it was a relief rather than a disappointment. At least now I had some understanding of the difficulties I'd experienced in school.

My father never realised his dream of a contented rural life. My mother's unhappiness in their marriage dominated his life and ours. On a number of occasions in my childhood she left him. She took us with her and we ended up staying in refuge centres. I remember we spent some weeks in a refuge on the Howth Road and a much shorter time at another in Mullingar. I could never understand why we'd up and leave so suddenly, but I knew better than to ask questions. And, in some funny way, there was a sense of adventure attached to those departures. We never went on family holidays so they offered a break from the normal routine. Perhaps more importantly, they meant I didn't have to go to school, which I dreaded more and more.

As an adult, I still don't understand why my mother would leave like that. My father wasn't a violent man. My parents certainly had their fights, and although they were both capable of striking out physically at each other, I know first-hand what it's like to be the victim of a violent relationship, and I never saw anything like that in my parents' marriage. Life was hard for both of them, and perhaps there were things I didn't see. Or perhaps it was simply her way of escaping for a short while from a man she despised. She always claimed that she was too good for him and that she should have married someone with a professional background.

I suppose my father had never known ordinary family life as a child and simply coped with the life my mother now offered him. But he always hoped that one day he would find his own mother, who had abandoned him. At one time, he must have received some information that would help him in his search, and I remember myself and Brian going with him in the car. It was summer and the day was hot. He stopped a few times to get directions and also called into the priest of whatever parish it was – I was too young to know. Eventually, he drew up outside a large old farmhouse. Brian and I stayed in the car. A woman came to the door and pulled it shut behind her. She had a brief conversation with my father as they walked towards the car. Then I watched her return to her house and close the door firmly behind her. My father didn't say much on the drive home to Coole. Later, I heard him telling my mother that this woman had her own family and had told him she'd had nothing to do with his birth. But he mentioned her eyes. They were blue, the same as his own, and it was the one feature that convinced him she knew more than she was willing to admit.

This rejection did not stop him hankering after his

past. On another occasion he took us to the convent in Drogheda where he was reared as a young child. He spoke to some of the nuns, who remembered him and allowed him to show us around. We saw the yard where he used to play and the particular corner he had to face if he misbehaved. Another time he brought us to Artane Industrial School. I imagined how he must have felt, leaving there one morning after he turned sixteen, then returning that same evening. He must have been so bewildered by the big city and the freedom stretching before him. I stared at the grim, high walls and imagined the stories they could tell if only they could talk.

I didn't finish my schooling, leaving at around fifteen, and I got a job potato picking in Meath with Dad. This was seasonal work and one of the many extra jobs he took on to earn a living wage. He'd wake me early in the morning and by the time I reached the kitchen he'd have a flask of cocoa made, along with a stack of blackcurrant-jam sandwiches. He'd buy a bottle of Lucozade on the way to the fields, and that would set us up for the day. I enjoyed working in the fields with him. It was hard but I was young and strong and did well at it. Nevertheless I was always waiting for the routine to change and for my mother to declare that we were on the move again after another explosive row.

My father had many jobs. He worked for Tom Tevlin, a prosperous farmer who lived near us, and also at Coolure House in Castlepollard as a general handyman, tending the gardens, doing the painting and decorating, and also helping to build a swimming pool. At the time this old Georgian house – built in 1776 for the younger brother of the Earl of Longford – was a holiday centre for young people, mainly catering for school groups and youth clubs from all backgrounds. It was run by the Catholic Youth Council, and Louis O'Neill was the manager. Separate units were available for families with troubled backgrounds, who could holiday there for a week. Lots of adventurous activities were available, including field sports, horse riding, cycling, swimming and canoeing. The trees were magnificent and were hung with Tarzan ropes and swings. My father was always ready to lend a hand with the canoes, or help out anywhere he was needed.

Louis O'Neill was one of the most generous and kind-hearted people I've ever met. He assisted our family in many ways. My father always appreciated his help. Occasionally, my mother worked on a casual basis at Coolure House and seemed to enjoy it. Once, she told me how she had put on music and danced in a big room with one particular young visitor. She laughed about it at home. It had been harmless fun, as far as she was concerned, but Louis O'Neill took a different view. One evening soon after, he called to our house. Usually he was in great form but on that night it was obvious that he was extremely angry about something. He pushed past us and told my mother that he wanted to talk privately to her. We were ordered out of the kitchen but we could still hear their raised voices. She never worked again at Coolure House and was very bitter about the experience. My father, who remained working there, took the brunt of her fury. There was nothing new in that, and life continued as usual until she informed me one morning that she was visiting a local doctor to discuss my father. I was to accompany her and to agree with everything she said. If I dared contradict her I'd be in serious trouble.

I accompanied her to Dr Cullen, who practised in the area but was not our regular GP. She cried in his surgery and told him she was terrified of my father's moods. I was fifteen at the time and wouldn't have dared deny anything she said. I remember walking back down Coole Hill with her and seeing a pink document in her hand. This, she said, would give her the authority to extend my father's stay in hospital, if necessary. At the time I'd no idea what was going to happen but I soon found out.

In March 1985, on the word of my mother, my father was committed to St Loman's Psychiatric Hospital in Mullingar. Guards were called to the house, and Louis O'Neill was also there. He objected to the order and said there was nothing wrong with my father, but the guards insisted on bringing him to hospital. Louis said, 'If that's the case then I'm going with him.'

Around that time, I had a crush on one of the local

lads, just innocent puppy love. His name was Anthony and the feeling was mutual. He bought me a ring, a cheap and cheerful piece of jewellery, and I was delighted with it. A few days after my dad entered St Loman's, we decided, along with a group of friends, to visit him. I don't think we had any sense of the seriousness of the situation or what it meant to be incarcerated in a mental hospital. All I knew was that I missed him and really wanted to see him. My mother went ballistic when I mentioned where we intended going. She pulled the ring from my finger, marched me to Anthony's house and made me give it back to him. I was then marched home and shoved into my bedroom. If I dared come out I'd get a hiding, she warned, and I was ordered never again even to think about visiting my father in hospital.

Louis O'Neill and Tom Tevlin were furious over the treatment he had received. After a week he was discharged and Tom Tevlin was there to collect him. My mother was equally angry as she had expected to determine how long he should stay in hospital. Tom had bought a cottage, which had been decorated to a high standard with the aim of renting it. It was empty at the time and he offered it free to my father for as long as he wanted it. I believe my father did stay there for a while but he eventually returned to us.

When he did, he was a beaten man, much quieter than before, and reluctant to mingle with the local community. He had spent his young years in institutions and this betrayal on my mother's part was too much for him to bear.

'Life is for the young and carefree,' my father once told John Kiernan, one of our neighbours, and that summed up his frame of mind. He was still a young man but he felt betrayed and degraded by his wife, who seemed determined to manipulate him and drive him out of his mind. I was about sixteen when she moved us to England, once again leaving my father behind. At first we stayed in a hostel in Crewe, then moved to Nantwich. The hostel was spacious and had great living and cooking facilities. During our time there my mother struck up a relationship with another man. She was happier in herself than I'd ever seen her, and she made no secret of the fact that she was having a good time. But she must have had second thoughts because she returned to Ireland on her own, leaving me in the hostel to mind the boys and keep everything going as best I could. I brought them to school and made sure they were fed.

The hostel was for homeless people, and I remember one family in particular whose house had burned down: they were living there while they waited for a new home. They were very good to us. My mother had left some money for groceries and other necessities so we managed to keep our heads above water. We waited some weeks for her return and she came back with my father. If memory serves me right, he wasn't entitled to stay in the hostel and my first sight of him was at the window: he was climbing into our room. He was delighted to see us and hugged and kissed us, and we were forced to keep down our excitement in case we were overheard by the management.

He found a job straight away, working on a motorway, and bought a car, a Morris Minor Traveller, which he later brought back to Ireland. We stayed in England for a short while before the decision was taken to return home. Before I knew it, we were back in Coole. One step forward and two steps back – that was the way their marriage worked. I felt like the pawn in the middle, never sure when the next row would explode around me, or where we would wind up from one week to the next.

We were only back home a short while before we left again, once more without my father. We returned to the hostel in Nantwich. During our stay there, a letter arrived from Dad. My mother had applied for an English divorce and he'd received the documents. He must have been convinced the break-up was final and he wrote a long letter to her, thirty-six pages in all, telling her he loved her and how much we all meant to him. Years later I read some pages of that heart-breaking letter and, knowing his lack of education, it must have taken a long time for him to put it together. He enclosed photographs of us with messages written on the back, pleading with us not to forget him.

It seemed as if a divorce was about to happen but as I tried to adjust to this new development in our lives, I discovered that my parents had decided to give their marriage another chance. By now I was seventeen and absolutely fed up with the pressures of being a surrogate mother to the boys while my parents tried to sort out their lives. I was tired of listening to arguments that went around in circles, tired of my mother ordering me around, of her moods and threatening silences, of always being in her shadow. I wanted to escape and find out who I was, to stand on my own two feet for once in my life.

I'd become friendly with Jimmy, an Irish-English lad whose Irish relatives were staying in the hostel. We'd go for walks together and talk to each other about our lives. He knew how unhappy I was and that I was thinking of running away. He suggested that I work for a woman he knew in Liverpool. She would give me digs for free if I did some jobs around the house for her. I was well used to hard work and I thought it was a great idea. Shortly afterwards, I left my family. I did not leave a note or any clues as to where I was going. It was a huge relief to leave everything behind.

My decision would profoundly change my life and set in motion events that have haunted me ever since.

Three

Meeting Colin Pinder

I arrived in Liverpool and met the woman as arranged. She had a daughter and I was given digs in return for cleaning the house and bringing her little girl to and from school. But it wasn't a good situation – the house was chaotic – and before long it became clear to me that it wasn't going to work out and I decided to leave.

I packed up my few belongings, and told the woman I was going for a walk. I kept walking until I found a Catholic church and a presbytery. The priest on duty listened to my story and offered to help. He made a few calls and found a place for me in a Salvation Army shelter for homeless people. Soon afterwards I got a job in a burger bar and was able to rent a small nearby flat.

It was my first taste of independent living. I wasn't frightened at being on my own in a big city but I was lonely. I missed my brothers and my father and longed for home. But I wasn't ready to return to my old life and I resisted contacting them.

I first met Colin Pinder when he came into the burger bar one day. I don't recall much about that first meeting, but soon afterwards he stopped me to talk when he recognised me in the road. It turned out that he lived on the street that ran parallel to mine. He invited me around. At first, our relationship was just friendly. He was into body building and boxing, and had converted his bedroom into a gym with a weights bench and dumbbells. A punch bag hung from the ceiling. He started teaching me how to do a workout. A nearby park had an obstacle course and we used to exercise there. I enjoyed getting my body into shape. At seventeen, I had serious issues about my weight and appearance, having been brought up on taunts that I was fat and ugly. Now I was beginning to see myself differently. Colin was also a good cook and often made me dinner when I'd finished work. He was five years older than me and I thought he was very sophisticated.

One evening I went back to my own flat and discovered that the door had been kicked in. My television was missing and my possessions had been flung all over the rooms. I ran over to Colin's and told him what had happened. When he saw the damage he offered to put me up for the night. He gave me his bed and he slept on the sofa. Our relationship moved on from there and I never returned to my flat again. During those months we were together, he taught me how to take care of my appearance, the kind of clothes and makeup that suited me. I had one dress in particular that was baggy and shapeless – no doubt bought to cover as much of my body as possible. He cut it up and stitched it roughly together to show me how I could look if I bought the right clothes. My confidence slowly grew as I emerged from the dowdy shadow I'd always believed was me.

I was still very innocent about the facts of life and had lots of hang-ups about intimacy. But Colin was patient and did his utmost to relax me when we finally made love. These were happy times and the future seemed blissful. Until the afternoon I looked out of his front bay window and saw my mother walking up the garden path. I found out later that both of my parents had come to England to find me, leaving my brothers in the care of a neighbour. They'd found the address of the woman I'd briefly worked for and traced me from there. But my mother arrived alone, and seeing her again brought all the old fears and anxieties rushing to the surface.

The bell rang and I begged Colin not to open the door. But she persisted, and when he finally answered it he told her I wasn't home. She said she'd call back. From behind the curtain, I watched her leave and tried to comfort myself with the belief that I had Colin to protect me. But the following day, when she arrived again, I knew we couldn't hold out. I hid in the bathroom and Colin brought her into the sitting room. I could hear her voice, and felt my new-found independence draining away with every word she spoke.

In the end I knew there was no escape. It was time to face the music. But nothing prepared me for what happened when we came face to face. Instead of launching into an offensive, she ran across the room and gave me a hug. This picture of a happy family reunion was, I quickly realised, a show for Colin's sake. She explained that the boys were with a neighbour at home but she never mentioned the fact that my father had come to Liverpool with her to search for me. I've no idea why she didn't tell me or why he didn't accompany her. I can only assume that she had decided to control the situation herself. Whatever the truth was, it quickly became clear that nothing had changed. Within a few minutes the familiar pattern of behaviour emerged.

In company, my mother had a habit of trying to make me look stupid and the person we were with feel like she and they were in some kind of exclusive club together. She'd say things like 'Veronica doesn't understand what I'm on about but you know, don't you?' She'd block me from the conversation as she spoke directly to the other person. Soon she was talking in this way to Colin, and I thought, Here we go again.

After a while, she got up to leave. It was clear that she wanted me back in Ireland and so did my father. I watched her walk away and thought of how I'd be drawn into the family bickering and tension if I went back – I hadn't realised how much I'd enjoyed being free until I'd spotted her walking up the driveway. I could see from Colin's expression that she'd impressed him. I suppose he'd expected some harridan to arrive, especially as I'd told him so much about her. But he'd met her when she was on her best behaviour. He said she wasn't like a mother at all, more like my older sister. If only she was, I thought, as we settled down for the evening. Then maybe I wouldn't feel I was always under her control.

She visited us once more and then returned home. But nothing was the same afterwards. We kept in touch by making arranged calls to the public phone box in Coole. She kept encouraging us to come over, even for a visit, and this sparked off the idea of our moving to Ireland. Despite my freedom, I missed my brothers, and I was anxious to see my father again. However, Colin was of mixed race, his mother white and his father Jamaican. I knew his father had had difficulties in England when he had married a white woman and Colin was afraid we might have the same problems when we arrived in Ireland. This was the late 1980s and Ireland was different then, especially in the countryside where people weren't used to seeing anyone who wasn't white. We discussed this possibility but I assured Colin we'd have no problems on that score.

Later, at his trial for my father's murder, Colin would accuse him of racism, but I can say with certainty that my dad was not a racist. It simply wasn't in his nature. In his younger days he'd worked on fishing boats and mixed with people of all backgrounds. His friends came from all over the world and I'd never heard him slag anyone off or put them down. I can say with a hand on my heart that he happily took in my boyfriend from day one.

The day we arrived, Dad was just leaving for work on a local dairy farm. He shook Colin's hand, kissed me and wished us well in our new life.

Before I came home, it had been arranged that we would live in a rented house down the road from the family home, but this arrangement fell through at the last minute. We'd no idea that this had happened until my mother led us around the side of our house and showed us a caravan. It had been lying empty on the grounds of Coolure House and my parents had organised for it to be towed onto our land. This meant we'd be living right beside her. I was very upset about the change of plan, especially as no one had mentioned it to us before we'd packed up and come to Ireland.

Colin looked around the caravan and returned to the house in a state of shock. He suffers with epilepsy and asked me to give him one of his tablets. As I was getting him a glass of water, he collapsed. It was the first time I'd witnessed an epileptic seizure and I was afraid he was going to die. But he came round and I helped him into one of the bedrooms. He slept for hours while I tried to adjust to the new arrangements. We'd no option but to move into the caravan so I had to hope for the best.

Colin stood out in Coole. He was impossible to miss, with his shock of curly black hair and dark complexion. My mother loved showing him off to friends and neighbours, and made no secret of the fact that she thought he was a handsome catch for her daughter. We drove to Coolure House one day where my father introduced him to members of the staff and took him all over the estate.

We decided to get married and this was a cause for celebration. I remember showing off my engagement ring and the excitement at home when we made the announcement. We'd only known each other a little over three months, but if my parents were worried about that, they didn't show it. My mother had eloped with my father and been married when she was eighteen so my age wasn't an issue. Plus my father, traditional in his ways, had felt uneasy about Colin and me living together before marriage, so he welcomed our news. We went together to our local pub, the Inny Inn, for a celebratory drink and he proudly introduced Colin to everyone in the bar as his future son-in-law.

The date for our marriage was set for a few months hence, 18 April 1987.

It was a night of family togetherness in an otherwise difficult atmosphere. Soon after moving back to Ireland, I was into the role of surrogate mother to my brothers again, who were aged around eleven, nine and seven. Much as I adored Brian, Andrew and John and loved being near them again, I didn't want to take on the mothering role. As for my parents, the rows were worse than ever and I soon regretted coming home.

My mother constantly intruded on Colin and myself, and I knew that in the long term we had to get away if we were to live our own lives. Being with my mother was non-stop drama. Everything seemed dependent on her moods, and I knew only too well how quickly they could change.

She never stopped talking about how she despised my father, and seemed to relish discussing with Colin the intimate details of her marriage. As usual, she would say, 'Veronica doesn't understand but you're a man. What's your opinion?' Her presence was a constant pressure and I was weary of listening to the same old complaints about her life in Coole.

After another row broke out in February, Dr Cullen was called to our house. My father was sitting by the range, and I remember him saying, 'I suppose you're here to send me on my summer holidays again.'

On that occasion Dr Cullen brought my father to

Coolure House where he was given a room for the night. I later heard that Dad was crying when he arrived, heartbroken at the possibility that he could again be separated from his home and family. On this occasion he was not committed, despite my mother's best efforts to stir up trouble. Soon he returned to us.

A family friend, Brendan McCabe, had space on his land in Corrylanna, a townland about two miles from the house in Coole, and he agreed that we could park the caravan there. My biggest worry was leaving my brothers behind: I felt it was my duty to protect them from the madness. But my own need to escape it was enormous – it was either that or crack up.

I finally made the decision to leave for Corrylanna after an almighty fight between my parents. A priest called Father Brendan Smyth had visited our home that day, the same man who, years later, was outed in court as a serial paedophile. It was not his first visit to us, and we had no idea of his notorious background or the scandal that would soon unfold. He never came to our house empty-handed, and he was always made welcome. He'd bring toys and sweets for the children, so needless to say there was great excitement. I never felt at ease with him. Something about his ways – he'd stroke my hair or stand too close for comfort – meant that I was always relieved when he left.

At the time Father Smyth was living in the Norbertine Order at Kilnacrott Abbey in Cavan, and he would often do the rounds of some of the families in the community, which is how my mother had befriended him. He was well aware of my parents' problems. He used to talk to them about their faith, how God would help to sort things out. On this particular day, he visited Coole in an effort to persuade them to take a short break from their family. This, he said, would benefit them and help them sort out their marital difficulties. I remember him sitting on the bench in our kitchen and setting out his plan. He'd stay in the house and look after the boys. I'd be able to help out too, and my parents could relax, knowing their children would be well cared for.

My father didn't agree. The more Brendan Smyth tried to persuade him, the more he argued against the idea. Looking back now, I wonder if he had sensed something, picked up on the clues that he would have recognised from his days in the care of a religious-run institution. Although he'd never spoken to us about abuse at the Artane Industrial School, the crimes committed there and at other such institutions are well known. He must have understood what could have happened if his family had been left alone with that man. And he didn't hold back on what he had to say to the priest. My father's behaviour was unusual. Under normal circumstances, he would never have insulted a priest. But whatever had sparked it, I'm eternally grateful that my brothers were not left in that man's care.

After Brendan Smyth left, another row broke out

between my parents. My mother was furious with my father for the way he'd behaved, and threatened to leave him again. My brothers were upset by the shouting and began to cry. But the row blazed on.

It was the final straw for me. Later that day Tom Tevlin came and towed our caravan over to Corrylanna. I settled quickly on the new site with Colin and loved the bit of distance we now had from my mother. It was great to get up in the morning and do our own thing. And my relationship with her improved now that she wasn't living in my ear and ordering me about. Colin and I were getting on well also. Although he missed Liverpool, he liked the country life. He brought the boys fishing to the Inny River, which is known for its pike, roach and bream, and it seemed as if our decision to come back to Ireland from Liverpool might work out. Also, we were looking forward to our wedding in April. It was going to be a quiet affair in the registry office in Mullingar.

Just days before my father was killed, myself and Colin called to the family home and I felt a familiar tension as soon as I went inside. Although no one said anything, I knew something had happened. We went in to him. My father was sitting on the bed in his room. I could see in his eyes that he was feeling very low. He was lonesome for his friend Louis O'Neill, who, tragically, had drowned while on holiday in France. His body had been recovered, brought back to Ireland and buried in Whitehall Cemetery a few miles away. With

Louis gone, my dad believed he'd not only lost a good friend, but also a protector, someone who had respected him and believed he was not the violent man my mother made him out to be. That night he gave out about how she always had time for other people but none for her husband. It was true: she treated visitors and guests with charm and kindness, which she never showed to him or to me. Despite his own unhappiness, he told me he still loved her and had loved her throughout his life. But he believed he'd lost respect in the village since his committal to St Loman's Psychiatric Hospital – and the latest episode when he had spent a night at Coolure House had totally undermined him. He no longer wanted to live where he was hated and despised.

I asked him not to leave us – I knew the boys would be upset – but he believed it was the only answer. He told me he was very proud of how I'd turned out and that he was sorry if he'd been hard on me when I was a child. Although I'd never doubted his love for me, he had been a strict father, not shy of doling out a wallop if I was bold or about to do something dangerous. But that was no more or less than most children received at that time if they misbehaved, and was far more lenient than the corporal punishment administered in schools. And it was nothing compared to the lashings I'd received from my mother. The main punishments my father meted out involved chores around the house or garden. It always struck me as strange how, when my mother had come from a loving, stable family background, she was unable to show love to me, while my father, brought up in institutions, was always a loving dad.

I'd caught Vera eavesdropping on the conversation when I'd gone out to make a cup of tea for my dad at one point, and it was clear from her face that she was fuming at what she'd heard. I've often wondered why she didn't let him go to start a new life of his own. It was, after all, what she had always claimed to want. But it was not to be. In the days to come another plan – a drastic one – took shape in her mind.

Four

The Night I Will Never Forget

During the two months Colin and I lived in the caravan, my mother left my father one last time and went to a refuge in Athlone. As usual, the row was eventually made up and she returned to Coole. Some time later, she called to the caravan one night. It was March and the evenings were lengthening, the weather beginning to soften. By now Colin was well aware of the intimate details of my parents' marriage. Or lack of intimacy: my mother had left him in no doubt that she no longer had a sexual relationship with her husband. She would ask him how a man could cope without a woman beside him and how was it possible for such a man or woman to relieve their sexual needs. She always made my father out to be a fool, too. I hated those embarrassing conversations. After she'd left, I'd talk to Colin and paint a true picture of my father, but I'd no idea which of us he believed.

On that particular night she entered the caravan on her own, although my father had accompanied her to Corrylanna. He went on to visit his friend, on whose land we were parked and whose house was close to the caravan. As usual she talked about my father, about his faults and how impossible he was to live with. At some point she said she wished he was dead. It was the only way she believed she could be free of him.

I thought back to my recent conversation with him, when he'd confided that he planned to leave her. Both Colin and I had spoken to him at length that night. He'd wished us well in our marriage and hoped we'd be happy. My mother had overheard us talking to him and had been annoyed that he was so open with us. I wished she could have applied the same logic when it came to herself.

She began to taunt Colin, telling him he wouldn't be man enough to do the job himself. This was more extreme than her usual wild talk, but not the first time I'd heard her make such threats. As always, she made no effort to involve me and soon my mind drifted off – my usual way of coping when she was in that mood.

Colin produced a spanner from among the tools we kept in a storage compartment in the caravan. It was a big one, the type that could be used for removing bolts from the wheel of a car. One blow would be enough, he said, and they started to laugh. Not for one instant did I take him seriously. Then my mother decided she wanted to know what my father was discussing with his friend and sent me to the house to find out what was going on. I've no idea what she and Colin talked about after I left the caravan.

I found my father and his friend chatting away together, and went back to the caravan to tell Colin and my mother to come up and join us, which they did.

Vera was in a giddy mood. She'd recently gotten into calisthenics and started showing off the movements she'd learned. My father was an unassuming man, and I could tell by his face that he was embarrassed by her display. When she saw that her behaviour was having the desired effect, she showed off even more, stretching and bending and twisting her body into different poses. But once she settled down the night passed off pleasantly with general chit-chat and cups of tea.

We said goodbye and left. It was a fine, bright night so Colin and I decided to walk back to Coole with my parents and have a cup of tea before heading back to the caravan. As we walked along the road I saw my mother make a gesture to Colin, as if they were exchanging a signal. Yet the conversation continued as normal.

When we arrived at the house we realised the door was locked. Neither of my parents had a key. The boys were fast asleep and we didn't want to wake them up. Mum and Dad began to argue as to who would climb in through one of the windows. Dad said she should volunteer as she'd been so keen to perform her calisthenics movements earlier. Sure enough, she was agile enough to make it through the window, and while we were waiting for her to let us in I noticed Colin take his hand from his pocket. Something slipped down his sleeve and he gripped it. I recognised the silver spanner he'd produced earlier in the caravan and immediately I gestured at him that he was not to have a fight with my father.

Sindy, our dog, used to torment the sheep in the fields beside us. To keep her out of trouble, we'd tie her up in the field when we went out anywhere. That night, unusually, she was barking non-stop, in a frenzy about something. I ran up the field to see what was wrong. I calmed her down and went back to where I had left Colin and my father. I was horrified to see my father lying on the ground at the back of the house. My mother came out the door with a slash hook and some other implement that might have been a wrench or a bar. She handed the slash hook to Colin and pushed past me. Everything was happening so fast that I'd only the vaguest impression of my father rising and running to the side of the house. I was panicking. I knew I had to stop the fight but I was horrified by the violence that had been unleashed. My father had grabbed a wooden ladder and was holding it in front of him, using it as a defence against Colin. It was clear that this was a vicious fight, but I told myself it would soon be over. It couldn't be anything more serious.

I saw my father fall to the ground. He must have been quite badly injured by then as he was resting awkwardly on his hip. He begged them to stop hitting him.

'Shut up,' my mother shouted. 'You never had any mercy for me for the last twenty-one odd years.' She hit him with the bar or wrench. Colin also shouted at him to shut up and the two of them continued to attack him. She turned to me and told me to go inside and turn up the radio. I knew she wanted to drown out the sounds of the fight. Her tone was hard and demanding: instantly obey or else. At this stage I was terrified that all the noise would wake up my brothers who would see what was going on. I hurried into the house and did as I was told.

Then my nerves gave way. I ran around to the steps at the front of the house and began rocking back and forth on the top step. Above me the sky was lit up, filled with stars. I prayed the fight would soon be over. I told myself the dust would settle, as it always did. No part of me could comprehend what was actually happening – that they were beating my father to death. I felt as if I'd left my body – I seemed to be watching everything from high above, no longer really there. I was looking down on myself, seeing myself shrinking into a tiny frightened child. The towering, gigantic trees, the moon filling the sky – the step where I was sitting seemed like a high ledge that would topple me forward if I tried to move. I cowered and rocked and prayed. I covered my ears, closed my eyes. I disappeared.

A while later, I've no idea how long, my mother came towards me and said something to the effect that he'd gone. Gone missing, I thought, and I was so relieved that he'd got away from them. In that same instant, I saw my father staggering down the driveway, his hands raised in the air, past the potato beds and rows of vegetables he'd planted, and out into the narrow side road with the ditches and hedgerows on either side. Colin ran up behind him with the slash hook. He caught my father on the back of his legs. I ran after them into the lane and saw my father standing in the ditch, trying to find shelter in the trees. Colin kept hitting the bushes with the slash hook but I ran past him and held my father.

He told me his eyes were stinging and he could hardly see in front of him. He begged me to stay with him. All I could do was hold him. 'You'll be all right if we stay together,' I assured him. 'Stay with me, Dad. Stay with me.'

I begged Colin to stop but he continued slashing at the bushes. My father made one last plea. He promised to go away for ever if they would just give him his car keys. They could have the house and everything he owned.

Next thing, my mother ran towards me and shoved me out of the way. A car was approaching on the main road, and she was frantic. We were only slightly off the road and it would look suspicious if the driver saw a group of people gathered together so late at night in such an isolated setting. She dragged me across the road, demanding that I stagger and pretend to be drunk. She shook me and dragged me from side to side, forcing me to stagger. I was terrified.

I prayed that the car would stop – the driver might be able to help or alert someone. But it passed without even slowing down. Once its lights faded, my father made a run from the ditch and struggled with Colin on the grass verge. He was wearing a heavy jacket, which he pulled off and flung at Colin. He tried to grab the slash hook but Colin and my mother held on to it and my father had to let go. He collapsed as he reached the gateway to the house.

He lay very still, his body curled up in a tight ball. His face looked distorted. Many years later in a courtroom I would discover that his skull had been badly fractured, which had been caused by blows inflicted while he was still alive. I ran towards the house, convinced he was dead. Next thing I remember, he was lying against the wall of the garage at the back of the house. They must have carried him in from the road. I remember seeing his blood splashed against the concrete bricks of the wall. I'll never forget the gurgling sound he made. I asked my mother what it meant and she calmly stated it was 'the death rattle'. Her earlier fear – when she had seen the car – had faded, and now she was very calm. At that point Colin lifted a concrete balustrade – my father made these and there were several scattered around the driveway – and brought it down on my father's head.

He was dead.

Something in me died too. Although it would take time before the full effects hit me, now I was trembling. I cried and prayed that I was having a nightmare and that I'd soon wake up safe in the caravan. My mother and Colin began to talk about what they would do with his body. Colin suggested they put him in a neighbour's slurry pit or in a bog. She said the bogs preserved bodies so that was out of the question. But no one would look on the person's own land for a body so she decided it would be safer to bury him in his field. She came out of the house carrying a grey blanket with a black stripe running down the centre of it. We'd got it from the local convent. My father had often said that he wanted a quiet funeral, no fuss, no bother. 'Just a blanket,' he used to say. 'That'll do the job instead of a fancy coffin.' As my mother flung the blanket on the ground, she said, 'You wanted a blanket, you bastard, and now you have one.'

They wrapped my father in it and carried him up to the corner at the far end of the field. They got shovels and began to dig. Vera was coolly issuing instructions to Colin. The light from the moon was bright, which worried her. They argued over how deep the hole should be and whether it would completely hide his remains. I believe they broke several shovels as they dug my father's grave. I walked around the house, or sat on the steps, afraid to go out, afraid to stay inside. Sindy knew something was amiss and was howling and barking non-stop. I went up to her and remember kneeling beside her, trying to stop her, terrified that the noise would wake up the boys, desperately trying to blot out what was going on around me in the darkness.

Eventually I returned to the house. The radio was still on in the kitchen. I'd always loved listening to Radio Luxembourg, but that night I knew I'd never want to hear it again. I don't remember sleeping but I must have nodded off on the sofa. I was awakened a short while later by my mother shaking me by the arm, saying that there was a big mess or things were bad outside. She handed me a blue hairbrush with white bristles, and a basin filled with water. My job, she told me, was to clear away the evidence from the bricks.

My father had built the garage and the concrete bricks had not yet been plastered over. As a result the blood and what must have been bits of flesh were embedded in the crevices. I was horrified and said I couldn't do it. She insisted. We had to clear away the evidence. Later, she described how she had hit him with a lump hammer, that Colin had ordered her to do it. I began to scrub but the more water I used the more the stains spread. Daylight was breaking and I could hear the dawn chorus. My mind was racing with a million conflicting thoughts. I was on my knees, sobbing, terrified my brothers would see me, terrified of my mother's anger, terrified a neighbour would call by and contact the police. Another part of me wanted badly to run to a neighbour's house and tell what had happened, get them to call the police. A split second later, thoughts of how the boys would react would fill my mind. How were they to respond to what had happened their beloved dad? It was too horrific to even think about. My thoughts raced back and forth in this way as I carried out my drastic task.

Vera remained cool and collected as she started to wash away the blood on the ground. I remember the red spreading out. Eventually, she went inside and took some ashes from the ashpit. She mixed them into the blood and the clean-up continued. When she realised it would be impossible to clear away the stains on the bricks, she covered them with lumps of tar. Thankfully, miraculously, the boys had stayed asleep throughout it all.

I've been asked many times why I didn't go to the police immediately, why I never told a soul. The truth is that I'd never realised the power my mother had over me until that dreadful night. What I'd thought was just another idle threat, another of her mad plans to get my father out of her life, had unfolded before my eyes. I'd been unable to prevent a murder taking place and I'd absolutely no idea what I should do next. I knew, even then, that I would never again have peace of mind. My father's life had been destroyed. And with it had gone part of mine.

Five

Trying to Carry On as Normal

The following morning, before the boys got up, my mother told me how she would explain their father's disappearance to them. She'd say he had left and gone to Holland to stay with friends while he looked for work. If I didn't go along with it, and if I ever told the truth about what had happened to anyone, she would have me admitted into the mental hospital and make sure I never got out again. She added that no one would believe a word I said anyway, but that if she was arrested, my brothers would be split up and sent to foster homes. I'd seen my father admitted to a psychiatric institution at her behest so I had no doubt that she would carry out her threat.

It's difficult to explain how I felt that morning. I was in deep shock. Things seemed unreal, as if I was still looking at them from a distance. All kinds of emotions were swirling around inside me, but I couldn't feel them properly. I knew that a terrible crime had been committed, something awful beyond words. I tried to think clearly about what to do, but my mind swung back and forth like a pendulum.

I knew keeping it secret was wrong. Yet my mother's threats played in my head. And I was worried sick about the boys. What would happen if they found out the truth? How could they comprehend that their father's remains were lying in a shallow grave and that their mother and my fiancé had put him there? Just when I'd convinced myself to disobey my mother and go to the guards, those thoughts would come into my head. I'd falter, and resolve to keep it secret.

Throughout the day, I tried to act normally. When my mother told the boys that their father had gone to Holland, and sent one of them to his place of work to collect his bicycle, I kept my head down and stayed silent.

My mother knew the boys wouldn't ask questions. It wasn't hard for them to believe their father had departed for Holland, where there was steady employment – and to them, moving from one place to the next was normal.

In the days following the murder, it was agony to pretend everything was okay. I don't know how any of

73

us did it. I spent the first day with Colin in Coole and returned to the caravan that night. For the first few days my mother and the boys also stayed elsewhere. We never discussed why she didn't stay in the house but I guessed she couldn't deal with what had happened there, especially at night.

I muddled through the next few days. As the sense of unreality left me and the true horror of what I had witnessed sank in, I found it increasingly difficult to cope – or to be with Colin. I tried to talk to him about the madness that had seized him that night, but I didn't get any clear answers. I don't honestly think he knew what had come over him. He said he'd been encouraged by my mother, that she'd taunted him about not being manly enough to take on my father. But that was only a lame excuse: she hadn't put a gun to his head. I found it hard to listen to his explanations. But the two of us were bound together by this terrible secret.

At some stage each day, we'd call to the house. My father had been an orderly man and, without his influence, the place was falling apart. Dishes lay piled in the sink, the floor went unswept, dirty clothes gathered in heaps on the chairs.

As the unbearable truth hit me that I would never see my dad again, I wished with all my heart that my mother's story about Holland was true. Part of me almost believed it. I kept expecting him to walk in the back door. One day I remember looking around the kitchen and saying to my mother, 'We'd better tidy up the place before Dad sees the mess it's in.'

She looked at me in amazement. 'Sure he won't be coming back here any more,' she said, and laughed. Nothing in her words or actions suggested that she felt any guilt or remorse over what she and Colin had done. If I tried to bring up the subject of my father's body lying in the field, she'd say matter-of-factly, 'When you're dead, you're dead. You're only a carcass.'

Trying to keep it locked inside me was the hardest part. I badly wanted to tell someone about what had happened. But I didn't have the courage. I was convinced I'd be locked away in a mental hospital while my mother went about her business as if nothing had happened.

She lost no time in building up the story of my dad's disappearance. She made arrangements to seek a barring order, and asked Colin to hit her so it would look as if her husband had roughed her up before he left. When he refused, she demanded that I give her a 'love bite' on the cheek. I felt sick at the idea but, frightened of what would happen if I refused, I did it.

With the 'bruise' in place, and looking quite obvious, I accompanied her to a solicitor in Granard where she applied for the order. We had to go to court to have it endorsed. She told the judge that her husband was violent and she couldn't take any more abuse from him. That she'd been in refuge centres for battered women must have added weight to her claim. That day she got what she wanted.

She also applied for the Deserted Wives' Allowance, which she duly received – and she claimed it until the day she was jailed for her husband's murder.

Everything was going according to her plan. She was dealing calmly with local people's questions about my father's disappearance. There was understandable curiosity as to why he'd left so suddenly. In a small community it's difficult to keep one's problems secret, and most people were aware that my parents had an unhappy marriage. But they kept to themselves their views on the subject, and accepted her excuses.

My mother was aware that the best way to keep suspicions at bay was for our lives to continue as normal. The boys were attending school, my wedding was going ahead and she, having sought a barring order and her Deserted Wives' Allowance, seemed to be putting a good face on her husband's desertion. I don't imagine anyone was surprised that Brian McGrath had finally packed up and left her.

The registry office in Mullingar was booked and Vera was determined that my marriage to Colin would go ahead as planned. When we'd got engaged, we'd been happy to tie the knot as soon as possible. We were young and in love – but everything was different now: I was living with a violent stranger. But although my feelings for him had changed, I didn't know how to end our relationship, especially with my mother demanding that we go ahead with the wedding.

I was worn down by her harping on at me, insisting on this, insisting on that, demanding that I pull myself together and stop making a show of her. I went along with the wedding for the sake of peace, and Colin was prepared to do the same. I can't imagine that, with everything that had happened, he saw a happy future for us. Or perhaps he believed we were safer together than apart: that way he could keep an eye on me, calm me down when I wanted to break the silence and confide in someone, anyone, who might be able to help.

My main memory of my wedding day is of quiet, numb despair. My mother came with us on the bus to the registry office. The boys were with us, and a family friend who would act as a witness. There was no fanfare, not even a dress, just an ordinary skirt, top and jacket. As we made our vows, promising to love and cherish each other, I fought down waves of nausea. Through the haze of that ceremony, one thought was clear in my mind: our marriage didn't stand a chance. Which of us would leave first remained to be seen.

Afterwards the celebrations were minimal, just sandwiches and a drink in the pub, courtesy of my mother. If I could have made one wish that day, it would have been for her and Colin Pinder to disappear for ever from my life.

We booked into a B&B for the night. I lay in the dark and remembered the wedding fantasies I'd had as a little girl: the exciting build-up to a special day, the bridesmaids and flowers and confetti, my dad walking me down the aisle, the romantic honeymoon. All gone now. I was in a different zone from my friends, old before my time, burdened with a terrible secret. I couldn't even discuss it with the man who slept beside me. Our conversations went in circles and usually ended up with us arguing and saying hurtful things. Already I could see the pattern of my parents' marriage forming in my own.

Obviously, in the weeks that had followed my father's death, there had been no passion, no romance. I felt disconnected from my surroundings, even from my own body. A kind of deadness would come over me when Colin touched me. Love had died and sex was something to be endured. I'd no way of expressing my feelings, too deeply shocked even to try to understand what I was going through, what had happened to both of us. I entered my own world, in which I could convince myself that my father hadn't been killed. He really *was* in Holland. Then I'd look out at the field and a terrible sickness would come over me.

Shortly after our wedding I discovered there was another reason for the sickness. I was pregnant. I watched each day for my period to arrive. When it didn't, I took a test and it came up positive. I was reeling from the shock. This should have been a joyous occasion, but it was impossible to imagine bringing a new life into our broken world.

The morning sickness was awful, made worse by my nerves. I felt weak and my head thumped. The stress of trying to act normally when I met neighbours in the shops, answering enquiries about my father, looking out at the field and knowing he was under the soil was taking its toll on me. I began having nightmares about his murder. Sometimes he was alive and pleading with me to save him; at other times he was dead and I'd wake up weeping.

With her barring order in place and her Deserted Wives' Allowance processed, my mother packed up again and went to England with the boys. She didn't tell me why she was leaving. Perhaps the house was getting to her and she needed to escape from the constant reminder that my father's remains were lying above in the field. She stayed initially at a refuge in London for homeless people, then moved into a council flat in Pinkholm House at Elephant and Castle.

I was still living with Colin in the caravan in Corrylanna. Once we heard she was leaving, Colin suggested moving into the empty house. I've no idea if they discussed this before my mother left, perhaps to make sure no one trespassed on the land, but there were other reasons too: the caravan was cold and damp, the atmosphere full of suppressed anger and depression. Also, Colin's epilepsy made it difficult to cope in such a small space. In the house, we would not be forced to confront each other every time we turned around. Reluctantly, I agreed.

By now any remnants of the love we once shared had well and truly gone. I couldn't stand the sight of Colin in the rooms where my father used to live, to see the empty chair at the range where he used to sit.

Many nights, I'd suffer a panic attack. The house would start to close in on me and I'd run out into the darkness, walk to the caravan and sleep there. 'Sleep' is not the right word: I'd spend most of the night tossing and turning, unable to escape my thoughts and fears. Sometimes Colin came with me, as if he, too, was unable to confront his ghosts.

One day, when Colin was busy in another room in the house, I decided to make a run for it. I packed a case as quickly as I could. I was going to make a new life, put as much space as possible between us. I wasn't thinking beyond the moment and had no idea where I was headed – or what I would do when I got there. I closed the case and checked that the coast was clear. There was silence in the house, and no sign of Colin – maybe he had gone out. I opened the front door and stepped outside, convinced that this was the last time I'd ever see Coole. I glanced towards my father's makeshift grave, then turned to the driveway.

I'd barely taken a few steps when Colin appeared at the door. He came running towards me, shouting at me to stop. He was furious. I kept going. But he caught me and dragged me back into the house by my hair. Inside, he picked up my guitar and smashed it into pieces. Then he began smashing dishes against the kitchen floor and wall. Beside himself with fury, he grabbed me and pulled me across the kitchen, laying into me as he went. It was only later that I felt the extent of the pain from the battering he gave me – the first and last time he ever laid a hand on me. He told me if I ever did anything like that again he'd dig up my father, put him on his back and drag him up and down the hill of Coole. I huddled against the kitchen wall, sobbing. I wanted to be dead and prayed to my father to help me. But I knew there was no easy way out for me. I'd witnessed a crime and I had to live with the consequences.

I held out the hope that someone else's suspicions would be raised – a neighbour might say something to the Gardaí. Or alarm bells might ring with someone in authority, my mother having disappeared so soon after seeking her barring order and applying for her Deserted Wives' Allowance. Questions would be asked. Although she had convinced me that I wouldn't be believed if I confided in anyone, I knew that if it came from outside me, there was a chance the truth would come to light. And I wouldn't stand in its way. I hoped and hoped – but the knock on the door never came.

My mother wrote every few days to check how everything was going. There was a phone box outside the post office in Coole and in her letters she'd tell us what time to expect her call. The code word for my father's body was 'the potatoes'.

'How are the potatoes in the field?' she'd ask. She

wanted to know if they were smelling, or if there were flies around the plot.

After those calls, as we made our way back to the house, Colin would go to the spot where my father was buried and check that everything was okay. I was shocked when he told me that parts of his body had begun to emerge from the grave.

About five weeks or so after my mother had left, she arrived home again with the boys. She hadn't told me she was coming and, if she'd told Colin, he hadn't mentioned it to me.

I know they were worried about my father's remains: there would soon be a smell of decay coming from the field and neighbours would be sure to notice. They immediately began to discuss what should be done. I wasn't a party to those conversations. She'd say, 'Colin, I want to talk to you alone,' and go with him into another room, or she'd tell me to get out of the kitchen so that she and Colin could have privacy. But I overheard certain details, picked up hints that were dropped, and was eventually told that a decision had been made. My father's body would be burned on a bonfire.

Bonfires in the country were not unusual then. People burned their rubbish, along with old, unwanted objects, and my father had lit many such fires in his field. We'd gather around, eat sweets, drink minerals, listen to stories. They were fun, and we always enjoyed watching the flames and the sparks flying. But this was no ordinary bonfire, and I was under strict instructions to look after my brothers in the house. The doors were to be kept locked and under no circumstances were they to be allowed near the field.

Six

The Burning of my Father's Body

Once the decision had been taken, the preparations began. Colin and my mother went up to the corner of the field and began to dig. The doors were locked, and the boys couldn't understand why they weren't allowed out. They were used to the freedom of the field, and as time passed, they became more agitated and impatient. They made a few attempts to escape from the house and I had to drag them back in. At one stage, I locked the door and ran up to the field to tell my mother I couldn't control them any longer.

When I got there, my father's shallow grave had been uncovered. Mounds of earth lay on either side of it and there was a putrid smell of decay, the like of which I'd never experienced. I fought the impulse to be sick. To the side of the grave my mother and Colin had dug another hole and filled it with four of the moulds my father had used for making the concrete balustrades. These were lined up dead straight, one behind another. The blanket that had been wrapped around my father had come away in places. To my horror I could see the outline of his body under a thin film of clay. His legs were visible and I recognised the trousers he'd been wearing that night.

Colin put his two hands under my father's body, lifted it up and laid it out on top of the moulds. The body was tiny and shrunken, almost unrecognisable. How Colin could lift him with his bare hands was beyond me. I can only imagine the state of hell he must have been in beneath his calm exterior – he and my mother looked like robots as they carried out their work. A decision had been made and they were determined to see it through to the end.

When I asked what was going to happen next, my mother ordered me to shut up and go back to the boys. I fought the waves of sickness and the tears, and thought about my brothers in the house, innocent and oblivious to what was happening. I had to take every precaution to prevent them going into the field. Somehow I held myself together and ran back to them.

Shortly afterwards, my mother and Colin came back to the house and began to collect briquettes, paraffin, and any rubbish that would burn. The old orange sofa that I lay on the night my father had died was added to the growing pile at the top of the field. By now the boys knew that a bonfire was being prepared and badly wanted to help build it. My mother warned them to stay away. They knew better than to argue with her, but they couldn't understand why they weren't allowed to help. I told them it was a dangerous fire, different from the ones we usually lit to burn rubbish.

Eventually, the pyre was set alight. Later, in court, Colin said it blazed for twenty-four hours. My recollection is that it lasted for three days and nights. At all times it was supervised by Colin or my mother. My father used to cut branches from the bushes that grew on three sides of the field. These were heaped in piles and added to the fire at intervals. The flames weren't visible from the house but as soon as we stepped outside we could see it glowing.

I cooked and cleaned and sent the boys to school in the mornings. In the afternoons I found ways to distract them. We'd recently got a video recorder and we got a lift into Castlepollard to the video rental shop. The boys' favourite action hero was Arnold Schwarzenegger and they played videos like *The Terminator* and *Commando* over and over. My mother had given me money to buy them sweets. We went for walks with the promise that we'd call into Dunleavy's, our local shop, for treats on the way back. But we could see the flames stretching skywards when we returned and they were annoyed at being kept away from the excitement.

On the second day I went up the field to complain that things were again getting out of hand in the house. I was running out of excuses to keep the boys away. Colin and my mother were piling the fire with the dead kindling my father had cut from the bushes. Colin had a pitchfork in his hand. They both looked exhausted, their clothes and hands marked with soot. On the ground I noticed a circular object that had fallen from the fire. Colin bent forward and tried to hook in on the end of the pitchfork. He missed a few times but, eventually, he caught it, lifted it and laid it back on the flames. It was glowing orange as it disappeared from sight. Instinctively, I knew it was my father's decapitated head. I tried to put it from my mind, but there is no banishing some images. It has haunted my nightmares to this day.

A pungent, sickening smell came from the fire. Years later I read a book about the Auschwitz concentration camp in Poland where more than a million men, women and children were put to their death during the Second World War. It must have been the same smell that came from the ovens where those innocent people perished. It was inside my nostrils, in my clothes, in my hair. It clung to the air, to the walls of the house, to Colin Pinder and to my mother. I couldn't bear them near me.

We didn't discuss what was happening. My brothers

remained in the dark and were excited when, on the last day, my mother came back to the house and told them they could go up and see the bonfire in its final hours. I was astonished. They grabbed their sweets and crisps and raced out the door and up the field, where they innocently played around the fire until the flames died away.

Later, Colin and my mother went through the ashes with a sieve, or 'riddle', a round piece of wood with mesh underneath. Any bones that wouldn't go through the sieve were put into a biscuit tin, and later transferred to the range in the kitchen to burn away, or else flushed down the toilet into the septic tank.

My father's passport was destroyed in the fire, along with his birth certificate and any other documents he had around the house. The heavy navy blue workman's jacket he'd flung at Colin in a desperate bid to defend himself on the night of his death also disappeared. It had been covered with blood. It seemed as if the last traces of Brian McGrath had been removed from this earth.

Seven

Making a Fresh Start

After my mother had returned from England, we had continued to live with her in the house. But the days of the easy chats between Colin and her, and her intimate confessions to him, were over. A new tension grew between them. She still spoke over me but now it was mainly to argue or find fault with him.

From the start, our marriage was on the rocks. I couldn't bear Colin to come near me. If he so much as touched me, all I could think was that his hands had killed my father. The truth of what had happened bound us together but also destroyed us.

My depression worsened and I began to let myself go. I stayed in bed for days on end, not even getting up to wash, not caring how I looked, or even if I lived or died. I went to my doctor. I longed to unburden myself and tell him the truth but I couldn't. I was prescribed a course of antidepressants. During that period, there were times when I can honestly say I was like a vegetable. I loved my brothers, but I could no longer feel the joy of loving them, or the sense of purpose – of being good at something – that had come from looking after them. I was dead inside, and the smallest thing was a struggle. Trying to answer their endless questions about when their dad would come home was heartbreaking.

My mother, on the other hand, was enjoying her new-found freedom. She went out dancing with a friend to the Bridge House Hotel in Tullamore. I couldn't believe she would show herself in public with another man. But then, to the rest of the world, and to her companion for that night, she was a deserted wife who deserved to have a good time, instead of staying at home waiting for her husband to return. This was the false world we lived in. My father had been murdered, his body incinerated – and she was carrying on as if she hadn't a care in the world.

But soon she had itchy feet again, and I knew that Colin also wanted out of Ireland. Now that their crime was well covered up, they were free to leave. We packed up and headed for London, where we moved into a council flat my mother had been allocated.

They might have wanted to leave the memory of my

father behind but the change of scene made no difference: his unseen presence was like an unspoken accusation. My brothers would ask after him, wondering if he'd been in touch and when he was coming to see them. Needless to say, my mother didn't encourage such questions. She and Colin argued all the time. Most nights I'd sit it out, teeth clenched, as they bickered over the smallest things. It was a repeat of how life had been with my father. We were all miserable.

I was now heavily pregnant and tried to concentrate on the baby I was carrying. Sometimes I would feel it move inside me, and forget my problems for a few minutes. I'd wonder if I was going to have a girl or a boy. I bought baby clothes and felt flashes of excitement. But once I was back in the flat, it was impossible to think about anything except why we were trying to build a new life in London. My mother had found work as a cashier in an amusement arcade on Walworth Road in Elephant and Castle. Colin had a job in the kitchens of a West End restaurant. I stayed at home and took care of the boys.

My due date, Christmas time, arrived, and on December 24 I went into labour and I was taken by ambulance to Guy's Hospital. Colin came with me, and my mother followed later. She asked the midwife if she could join us in the delivery suite. Neither Colin nor I wanted her to be present at the birth and he went outside to talk to her. I could hear them arguing, each one trying to have the last word, and soon it had broken into a shouting match. When Colin came back he was stressed out, but he'd got his way. By now, I was beyond caring. I was in the midst of a long labour, and the baby wasn't budging.

Suddenly, Colin toppled forward into a seizure, crashing into some of the machinery. There was uproar among the medical staff. But at least he was with skilled people who brought him safely through it. He was black and blue when he recovered but he was also the father of a strong, healthy thirteen-pound baby boy. We named him Liam. I was discharged a few hours later from the hospital, despite my difficult labour, and a nurse came to the flat a few days afterwards to remove my stitches.

Right from the get-go, my mother tried to take over with Liam. She'd given birth to four children and insisted she knew the right way to do everything. And she made it perfectly clear that it wasn't the way I was doing things. Admittedly, she had experience of dealing with small babies, but I'd done my fair share of looking after the boys when they were babies too, so I was quite confident with Liam. I was determined to do things my way. I had decided to breastfeed and, more than anything, I wanted calm around me. I tried to keep the peace between my mother and Colin, but it was impossible. He hated the way she wanted to control everything, especially Liam, and she was moody and unpredictable, which he also found hard to cope with. As usual, I was piggy in the middle, and when I did express an opinion it was either ignored or shouted down.

Looking back I wish I'd had the guts to stand up to them, to scream at them to leave me alone, as I did in my mind so many times. But in their company I was tongue-tied – and scared. They were two dominant people and I'd seen exactly what they were capable of doing. They fought over trivial things. My mother would turn the heating down and Colin would turn it up again. She'd insist he hand his wages over to her every week and, no matter how much he gave her, she'd claim it wasn't enough and demand more. He worked long hours at the restaurant but had very little to show for it at the end of the week. She was using the same tactics on my husband as she had used on her own, even expecting him to pay for her driving lessons.

I did my best to look after Liam and the three boys while she was in work. But I could barely look after myself. And Liam wasn't the easiest baby to handle. He suffered badly with colic and cried day and night. One night I was so distraught from trying to calm him down that when I went to put gripe water on his soother, I let the bottle slip and accidentally spilled the liquid over his little face. I was trembling as I tried to dry him off, crying my eyes out. I cried a lot then – and once I started, I couldn't stop, sometimes not for hours.

As the atmosphere in the flat worsened, my mother took to her bed claiming to be depressed. This was nothing new. She had severe mood swings – giddy and laughing, then dark and brooding. Neighbours back home had at times been puzzled as to how she could be totally withdrawn one minute, then madly exercising the next. On this occasion she stayed in bed for days on end. The tension between her and Colin had reached fever pitch, and by now they weren't speaking. Colin had bought in some drink for Christmas and there was beer in the fridge. She ordered the boys to keep her supplied. All day long they went in with drinks and came out with empty glasses or bottles. My mother had never before been a drinker, and I was amazed at this turn of events. I later discovered that she was emptying the glasses and bottles out the window just to annoy Colin. This was obviously her way of getting attention, even if it was only to have an argument.

She had other ways of demanding attention. She'd play music at full blast at two or three in the morning or, during the day, turn up the radio so loud that we couldn't hear ourselves think. She admitted that she did this to drive Colin mad. She might have succeeded – and not just with Colin. She had also started going out with men and her old habit of talking about sex, not caring who heard her, got worse. I was at the end of my tether.

When we couldn't take any more, Colin and I decided to go back to Ireland with the baby. She was furious when she heard and insisted that she wouldn't be able to cope with the boys on her own. My first thoughts had always been for my brothers, but now I had my own child to look after, and that was struggle enough. I'd made up my mind. We were leaving.

First we decided to visit Colin's parents in Liverpool to introduce them to their new grandchild. We stayed for four days. I liked Colin's father, who was courteous and kind to me. I was interested to discover that he'd arrived in England from Jamaica with his mother, who was a lone parent. She'd been unable to look after him and, like my own father, he had been reared in an industrial school. He'd had a hard life and suffered from racial abuse when he was growing up.

When we reached Coole, I was astonished to see that my mother was already at home. She had packed as soon as we had left and followed us, expecting us to be there when she returned. She demanded to know where we'd been. My heart sank into my boots. Colin's mood had lifted over the few days we were away from her, but I knew what was in store now that she was back on the scene. More upsets and crazy behaviour.

Things went from bad to worse and the atmosphere between Colin and my mother was very strained. After a particularly ferocious row one day between them, I discovered Colin unconscious on the bed and realised he'd taken an overdose of his epilepsy medication. He was still breathing but I'd no idea if he'd swallowed enough to kill himself. I ran to my mother and told her what had happened. She was furious. She insisted he'd be all right and we should let him sleep it off. She stormed out of the house in a temper. By now my brothers knew that he had taken an overdose and were as frightened as I was. We'd no means of transport to get him to hospital or a phone to call an ambulance. Luckily, a family friend dropped in and I told him. He immediately got Colin into his car and drove him to Mullingar Hospital. He was kept in overnight and discharged himself the following morning.

When he got home he didn't want to talk about the incident. Words weren't necessary: he'd done what I'd wanted to do many times since the night of the murder. We continued to struggle on. My mother was careful around him now – she didn't want a repeat of that row. She knew he had difficulty sleeping and gave him sleeping tablets. But the tensions simmered away, barely beneath the surface, and I never knew when things would erupt.

Eventually, after another massive row, Colin, Liam and I moved out again. We hitched into Castlepollard, where I'd attended the vocational school, and asked in a pub if there were any places to rent. When no one knew of any, Colin became convinced that his skin colour was to blame. Then someone remembered a flat not far away that might be worth checking out. I left Colin minding Liam in the pub and went there. It was small and cramped but we didn't have any choice so I agreed we'd take it. We moved in immediately.

There was a problem with that flat. Rats. I was familiar with the sight of them – but they had been in fields or ditches around Coole. Seeing one running across the kitchen floor was another matter, especially since it looked as big as a cat. And where there was one, there were more. Traps and poison made no difference. I was worried about Liam's health, afraid he'd get bitten and catch Weil's disease. I'd stamp my feet and shout before entering any of the rooms. It was a horrible way to live but we tried to put up with the conditions rather than return to my mother. As it was, every time she called to see us, there'd be another blazing row between her and Colin, or she'd fight with me over how I was looking after Liam.

No matter where we went, my father's ghost was never far away. We never talked about what lay behind the problems in our relationship, but we bickered all the time. Colin became less and less able to function. He'd sleep most of the day and toss through the night. It was a shut-down situation for both of us.

It's hard to know how we managed to stay married for a week, let alone almost two years. But these things are rarely straightforward. Even though I no longer loved him, I'd become dependent on his support. He understood why I was depressed, just as I understood how he was feeling. There was no pretence between us, and the busy months when Liam was small and needy held us together.

He was also the buffer between my mother and me: her anger was now mainly directed at him. Our misery was obvious and we endured our lives because we didn't know what else to do.

Colin was the first to break away. He told me he was going back to England to find work and a proper place for us to live. I knew we couldn't continue living with a baby in a rat-infested flat and I believed what he said. With him gone, I'd have to cope on my own with my mother.

I handed the keys of the flat to its owner and once again moved back to Coole. I prayed it would only be a few days before I could leave again.

Eight

Coping Without Colin Pinder

After he left, Colin wrote each week from London and arranged a time for us to talk at the telephone box in Coole. The letters and calls continued for a few weeks. He'd explain how he was still looking for work and hoped to have a flat for us as soon as he'd settled down. I longed for the call that would tell me everything was arranged and I could leave Coole behind me for ever.

Then his calls and letters stopped. Every morning I'd watch for the postman, hoping for a letter with an English stamp. I'd be disappointed, then begin the long wait until the next day's post. I'd no way of getting in touch with Colin, no phone number or even an address. As the weeks passed, I grew more uneasy and, though I wasn't really surprised – we'd known our marriage was over before it had begun – I was scared. Without Colin, I would have to look after a young child by myself, which would make me more dependent than ever on my mother.

Life in Coole was a nightmare. At this time, my mother was seeing a man with whom she had begun a relationship shortly after my father's murder. I couldn't believe she had the nerve to get involved with someone else after what had happened but, as she saw it, she was free to do as she liked. She continued to take care of her appearance, always making sure she looked her best for him. My appearance, on the other hand, was the last thing on my mind.

Around this time, she decided to sell the house and a For-Sale sign arrived. She soon discovered that this wouldn't be as straightforward as she'd thought. The house was in both my parents' names and, even as a 'deserted' wife, she couldn't sell without my father's permission. She was frustrated by this but it didn't break her resolve to leave the house in Coole. She decided to move to Navan and rent a private house in Belcourt Estate. She sold most of our furniture and anything else she could lay hands on that would make extra money to pay the deposit. After moving to Navan, she joined a number of support services for lone parents and applied for a council house.

After about a year had passed, it was clear that Colin had deserted Liam and me. Unable to believe he would leave us to manage alone, I decided to go to Liverpool to track him down. I took Liam, who was a little under two years old, with me and called to Colin's family home.

His mother looked shocked to see us when she opened the door. She invited us in but it was clear that we were not welcome. She told me she'd no idea where Colin was living. I didn't believe her and insisted that she give me an address. She must have realised how desperate I was because, in the end, she showed me a letter she'd received from him. In it, he told her he'd moved on with his life and had met another woman. He wrote that he was sending maintenance money to me. That was a lie. I hadn't received a penny from him. Perhaps his mother was worried that I'd demand assistance from her – I don't know – but it was obvious that she wanted me to go home to Coole as soon as possible.

She agreed to put us up for one night and paid our fare back to Ireland. Colin's father treated me kindly but I knew from the looks his wife gave him that he was not to encourage me to linger. Nor did I. The following day I returned to Ireland. Unlike my mother, I was now a genuinely deserted wife. It was only years later that it occurred to me, I was the one who should have been getting the Deserted Wives' Allowance – I genuinely was a deserted wife, but it never even once occurred to me to apply for it.

When my mother was settled in Navan, she became

a child-minder and looked after children in their own homes. I continued to care for my brothers and Liam. All the children were growing up: in Coole they'd had the freedom of the country to run off their energy but now we were living in a large town. I warned my mother that my brothers needed more supervision than I could give them.

By now she had met yet another man and was very keen on him. For some reason she told him her name was Sara and we had to remember to address her by that name. Evidently she didn't want him to know she was a grandmother so she introduced me to him as a young single mother she'd picked up on the street, a homeless waif with lots of issues. I'd issues all right – and the main one was standing right beside me. I'd listen to her telling these barefaced lies without the slightest sign of embarrassment. She was in Fantasy Land, in love, obsessed. If this man didn't ring or turn up for a date she'd break down crying and I'd find myself comforting her, hoping to God he'd get in touch before she drove me crazy.

When the council offered her a house, she lost no time in moving into it. I worked out that I could just about afford the rent on the house where we were living. At various times I'd worked in a café in Navan town centre and done some house cleaning, so I'd managed to put some money into the Credit Union. My father had instilled in me the habit of saving and I hoped that some day I'd buy a small place for myself and Liam.

I succeeded when I was twenty-one. Thanks to my father, I had managed to save a thousand Irish punts and discovered that some old council cottages were for sale in Navan on St Patrick's Terrace. They were very basic, with boarded-up windows, no bathrooms or toilets, just two small bedrooms, a kitchen and living room. When I enquired about the guide price I was told to write my best offer on a piece of paper and drop it into the auctioneer's office. After that, I had to hope for the best. The highest offers would secure houses. I decided on £700. A week later I got a letter saying it had been accepted. I couldn't believe it. I was thrilled to have a place I could call my own. Although it would be a long time before proper repairs could be made, I was now a property owner and could afford to wait. If I continued saving, I could provide Liam with the stability I never had as a child. The only snag was that once I purchased the house, I would no longer be eligible for a council house.

I was lonely. I needed company, someone who could make me laugh again. I met Tom, a car mechanic, at a First Holy Communion party my friend was having for her son. Though he was ten years older than me, we enjoyed each other's company and became friends. I liked the companionship but I wasn't looking for a serious relationship. Gradually, though, we became closer. My mother used to babysit when we went out together, in return for cigarettes and drink. If money was too tight to get them for her, I'd have to cancel the date.

Tom still lived in his family home. His mother, Mary, was lovely and we got on well. She fulfilled my idea of the perfect mother: warm, affectionate and natural. The teapot was always hot when I entered her house and she made sure I'd something to eat. She'd married Tom's father when she was very young. He was a widower with a large family and she'd reared his children as well as their own family. Sadly, she died of cancer but I've always remembered her fondly.

After some time with Tom, I discovered I was pregnant again. I was devastated. I was only barely keeping my head above water. More importantly, I knew I wasn't in love with him, or he with me. We had been together for around three years and the arrangement had suited us both for as long as it lasted. But now we were faced with a momentous decision and he made no secret of his feelings. We'd been friends and lovers, and now we decided to go our separate ways.

I couldn't afford the repairs on my house and paying rent on the private house was no longer an option. I needed to put every penny I could spare into making my new home habitable. For the time being I had to live with my mother again in Navan. As my pregnancy advanced, my depression returned and got worse. I believed I was too unstable to be a proper mother. I had little means of my own, no outside support and no possibility of moving into my own house until I had saved for the necessary repairs and had them done. That seemed a long way off. How could I look after two children and rear them in a home where my mother and I were living a lie?

I didn't realise how important my relationship with Tom had been until it had ended. I'm not talking about love or dependence, although there had been elements of both at times, but when we were together it was like having a bandage to cover a wound. My mood would lift and life no longer seemed so dark. He offered an escape from the conflict between myself and my mother. But now, with a baby on the way and a little boy to look after, everything had changed. My mother seemed more demanding than ever but, looking back, I was probably just less able to cope with her moods. I snapped easily, as did she, and, as the months passed, I sank further into that black hole.

I was beset by fears, terrified of the dark. Memories I had suppressed came back to haunt me in my dreams. I had a recurrent nightmare featuring Colin Pinder at my father's bonfire, a pitchfork in his hand, and my father's head, glowing orange. In my nightmare Colin ran around the field, the head held aloft on the pitchfork, as he and my mother laughed. Every night, I woke up sweating.

Feeling I had no alternative, I made the painful choice to have my baby adopted. Although I felt very sad about my decision, the thought of bringing another child into such a chaotic, dysfunctional world was worse. My mother was totally against this plan. We argued over it but my mind was made up. As my due date drew nearer, the ache inside me deepened, but I kept my mind focused on what I felt was the only realistic option for me.

When I went into labour and arrived at the maternity hospital in Drogheda, I told the staff I was on my own and that I had another child from my failed marriage. I wanted to be honest with the nuns, who ran the hospital, from the beginning. I was afraid they would frown on me for my behaviour but, thankfully, they were very understanding and I was given my own room. They had arranged for an adoption agency to meet me and I'd signed the papers before my baby was born.

My second son was born in 10 June 1990. I called him Bernard, after my father, who was also known by that name. That August I would be twenty-two and I felt as if I'd lived way beyond my years. I looked out the window, beyond the hospital, to the grounds of the convent where my father had spent time as a young, abandoned child. I thought about the industrial school in Artane and how much he'd hated his time there. The tears started to flow. At that moment my mother arrived, dressed up to the nines. She sat down and ordered me to fetch her a cup of tea. It was only hours since I'd given birth and, still weak, I went into the corridor to ask someone. I was promptly ordered back to bed, and when I returned my mother was holding Bernard. Again, she tried to persuade me to keep him. But I had made my decision. We were a dysfunctional family and I was determined to give him a better life than I could give him. Now I just wanted to get it over with. We took some photographs so that I'd always remember what Bernard looked like when he was born. My heart was breaking as, the following day, I handed him over to the nuns.

I went home and spent that evening crying. The pain I felt inside was indescribable. Bernard had been in my life for such a short time but the bond I felt with him ran so deep. And now I would never see him again, never know what he was like growing up, going to school, making his First Holy Communion, all the special events that a mother shares with her child. As the hours passed, I knew I couldn't let him go. No matter how hard it would be to cope, I had to go back to the hospital and take my child home.

My mother was delighted. We forgot our differences as we planned what to do. The adoption papers were signed so we had to act quickly. I had no pram, nothing to wheel him from the hospital. One of my brothers went off and brought back a Londis shopping trolley. We padded it with blankets and I went to the hospital with my mother. I told the nurse I'd changed my mind and, to my surprise, the nuns were delighted. My mother dressed Bernard and we took him home.

That night I was so relieved I hadn't let him go to another family. I hugged him tightly and felt immense love for him. I knew I'd made the right decision.

The next day we went into Navan and bought a Moses basket and everything else we needed for the baby. I felt as though this child had come into my life for a reason. I had to do what was best for my children and that meant making life as good as possible for both of them.

Nine

Leaving for Liverpool

Depression is difficult to explain to someone who has never suffered from it. In my case, the need to unburden my terrible secret was like a constant pressure against my forehead and a major contributor to my illness. In the year following Bernard's birth I wouldn't go outside the house unless I absolutely had to. I became addicted to Valium, which helped me gather the courage to walk out the door. I took no notice of my surroundings – I could have been living in a palace or a hovel, it would have made no difference to how I felt. The headaches and the nightmares dominated my life. I stayed in my pyjamas all day long.

My mother suggested that a course of Prozac would

109

solve the problem, so I saw a doctor, who diagnosed post-natal depression. There was probably some truth in that, even though I had been depressed long before Bernard's birth. It was also the second time for me that an important relationship had failed, and it seemed even harder to deal with this time. Unusually, my mother was not without compassion. Some nights when I was unable to sleep, she'd come downstairs to the kitchen and sit with me. She'd listen to my worries but, eventually, she'd become frustrated when I couldn't respond to her. Unlike me, she was energetic, anxious to get on with her life and enjoy the freedom my father's death had given her. I was a weight around her neck, a constant reminder that she had no right to that freedom.

I remember sitting in the house one day and looking at my cigarettes on the mantelpiece. I badly wanted one but the packet was just beyond my arm's reach. I hadn't the strength to get up. The lack of energy, physical and mental, was stronger than my craving for a smoke. My mind and body were shutting down. I'd come away from the doctor with a prescription for Prozac, but what I really needed was a counsellor, someone in whom I could confide. I thought of going to England and building a new life with my sons. But I was in no fit state to manage on my own.

Somehow, with the help of the medication, I began eventually to pull myself together. I started going out again, to a film or for a cup of coffee, or just taking my boys for a walk. For the first time since my father's death it seemed that I'd found some peace of mind, and I resolved to try to leave the past behind. My mother encouraged me to look to the future. We were getting on reasonably well, without the constant tension that had defined our relationship in the past.

We were out walking together one day when we passed a bungalow with a car outside that had a For-Sale notice attached to its window. My mother was keen to buy a car and decided to make enquiries. An older man answered the door and talked to her about it. She decided against buying it but he invited us in for a cup of tea, and that was the start of a new friendship. We'd often call into Philip for a chat or he'd drop into our house to see how we were getting on.

The friendship continued over the following months. Tensions had heightened again at home. We were still living in Navan and I was finding it tough coping with two small boys in such cramped conditions. When I mentioned it to Philip he suggested that the boys and I move in with him. At first I was nervous about taking him up on his offer. My history with men hadn't been great and I didn't want to make the same mistakes again. Philip was a more mature man, though, more than twenty years older than me, dependable and protective. I felt I could rely on him. But I still hesitated.

One evening another row erupted at home and I decided enough was enough. I put the two boys into the pram and grabbed as many of our things as I could carry. My mother pleaded with me not to go, running up the road after me and begging me not to move in with Philip. But I was determined to break away, once and for all.

In the beginning Philip and I got on well. There was plenty of space in the bungalow, and a garden for Liam to play in. But Philip was used to having his own space, and I was conscious of our noisy invasion. And the age difference sometimes made me feel like a child, unable to express my own opinions. I could feel myself being dragged down into the depression that I had recently climbed out of, and I dreaded returning to that hopeless black emptiness. Men weren't the solution. I needed to strike out on my own.

On one occasion I decided to return to Coole with my two sons and live there until I sorted out what I would do with my future. My mother and brothers were still living in Navan, and although the house in Coole had become rough and ready, I knew I'd soon get it into order. We settled down and I enrolled Liam, who was about four at the time, into the national school. I'd no car so getting around was difficult but I managed as best I could. I'd a lot to think about, and being back at Coole brought memories of my father's death more forcefully to mind. When I was getting on with my life elsewhere I could dull them with anti-depressants but that was impossible once I was back at home. Yet the house was my refuge when I had nowhere else to go. I'd try to block out the bad memories and think about the good ones – and there had been good times between the turmoil and rows that had dogged my parents' marriage.

I wondered, living back here, if I had the mental strength to break away completely and manage as a single mum. My own relationships had not been easy. Two fathers who would not know their children, and Philip, who had offered me a roof and companionship when things became impossible between myself and Vera. I depended on him, just as I'd depended on the others, for protection and an escape from the past.

I knew I was too reliant on antidepressants to get me through the days. They only helped to a certain degree, unless I upped the dosage, which meant becoming even more dependent on prescription drugs. I wondered what to do. Where to go. How to forget. I'd look out at the field and remember. I'd sleep at night and my dreams were memories. My anger with Colin Pinder grew stronger. I cursed the day we'd met, the day we'd made the decision to come to Ireland. I didn't want him in my life again but I needed to understand what had happened that night, what had triggered the merciless rage, the savagery, that had caused him to lift a balustrade and crash it down on my father's head. I thought about my mother's fury, the weapons she'd handed Colin, the blows she'd struck, them digging the grave, the fire burning weeks later. I knew those had been desperate acts, prompted by the need to hide the crime, taking her and Colin to a dark, demonic place in their minds. And I had seen it all. I had been a witness to evil and had failed to stop the carnage.

The person who angered me most was myself. When I was alone, without the support of a protective man, I was filled with self-loathing, not caring if I washed or combed my hair, if I never changed my clothes or cleaned my teeth. The person who stared back at me from the mirror reflected the darkness of my thoughts.

In such a small community as ours, my father's abrupt departure was bound to be discussed eventually. His family had meant everything to him and, as time passed, people must have wondered, as my brothers did, why he never came back to visit or made arrangements for us to visit him. Shortly after his disappearance, one of our neighbours, Michael White, was doing some repairs to his own boundaries when he noticed the loose clay from a freshly dug plot at the top of our field. It was oblong, the shape of a grave, and he wondered if we'd buried an animal. We always kept dogs, chickens and a few goats. Like the rest of the local community, he'd heard that my father had gone to work in Holland but the thought did cross his mind that Brian McGrath might be buried in that plot. He dismissed his suspicions as ridiculous and was afraid that if he went to the guards, and they started to dig on the land, they'd end up finding the carcass of an old goat.

As the years passed, and my father made no effort to contact his family, there was a certain amount of speculation about what had become of Brian McGrath. People don't disappear into thin air, John Kiernan often thought, when he called into our house and looked towards the chair by the range where my father had always sat. One theory was that he might have drowned in the Inny River. It's deep, varying from one and a half to three metres, and there had been drownings in the past. But John always believed that if such a tragedy had occurred, my dad's body would have floated to the surface or snagged at some point on its journey to the Shannon. John had spoken to my father in St Loman's and knew he was very unhappy with how he was committed. Years later, during my father's murder trial, John would testify that he had confronted Dr Cullen in 1989 about my father's committal. 'I challenged him with putting in Brian McGrath,' he said and told the court that he had always had his suspicions about my father's disappearance. 'I told the doctor he was a missing man,' he said, and that my father was responsible for 'putting bread on the table for those children'.

People also wondered why, if Brian McGrath was living abroad and was known to move to wherever the work took him, he had not been seen by friends or acquaintances on any of the building sites or road constructions across the UK. But rumour was one thing, fact another, and there was no clue that would lead anyone to the truth – that there was a more sinister reason behind his disappearance.

My mother must have heard that I'd returned to Coole. She arrived one evening carrying a box of groceries. She was wearing a beautiful red dress, her hair was freshly done and she looked a million dollars. The contrast between us was stark. I could tell immediately that she was spoiling for a fight. She hated to see me in a mess when she was in top form. I was a drag on her – or maybe I was her conscience, a constant reminder of the past she wanted to put behind her.

My brothers were in the house with her, caught as always between the two of us, unable to understand why I was such a mess and she was always so angry with me. She said she felt like someone from the St Vincent de Paul Society handing out charity to me and my sons. She made the usual comments about pulling myself together and getting on with my life. I was holding her back – I could see that at a glance. A terrible anger came over me that night as I listened to her. The pressure of all the thoughts that had been spinning around in my mind was unbearable.

'Where's our father?' I yelled at her. 'Don't you think you should tell the boys where their father is?' I felt as if the words had been torn out of me.

'Why don't *you* tell them?' she shouted back and, for an instant, I wanted to let it all out, there and then. But I looked at their faces, the innocence of their expressions, and I knew I couldn't bring myself to say the words.

Vera was beside herself with rage that I'd dared to challenge the story that she had been deserted. I was ordered out of the house with my children. She followed me out to the driveway and down the lane, and warned me never to come back.

By now it was late in the evening and cars were parked outside the local pub. I thought of calling in and seeing if I could hitch a lift but I was too embarrassed – especially as I'd no idea where I was going. It was my first experience of homelessness and it was frightening.

At the time we had a dog called Prince. He followed me from the house and kept walking beside us, no matter how many times I ordered him to go back. He was a distraction for the boys in the beginning, but I still had to jolly them along. When I reached the public phone in Coole, I knew I had to do something to get us shelter, even if it meant ignoring my pride and asking for help. I had a phone card with a few units left on it. I rang Philip and told him I'd had a row with my mother. We hadn't been in touch since we'd parted but he said immediately that he would come and collect me.

We arranged to meet at a certain house and I started walking towards it. By now the boys were hungry, cranky and tired. I had Bernard in my arms but Liam also wanted to be carried. I threw our possessions over a ditch, lifted him in my arms and carried them to the house. I was wearing a long coat and I used it to keep the boys warm until Philip arrived. Eventually the lights of his car lit up the darkness and we climbed into the warm seats.

The small house I'd bought a couple of years earlier remained boarded up. I'd never accumulated enough money to do the repairs. But I was determined this time that I wouldn't return to my mother. Instead I decided to seek help in a women's refuge in Navan. They found a place for us in another refuge in Athlone, to which we moved in 1993.

We had a family room in the hostel and I shared a kitchen with a number of others. Living in a hostel and sharing a communal life wasn't new to me. I'd become used to it when I was younger and I knew almost by heart most of the sad stories I'd hear.

I wanted to put as much space as I could between myself and my mother so I talked to the people who ran the hostel about the possibility of moving to England. I'd once lived in Liverpool so that seemed the obvious place to go. But I had another reason for choosing that city: I wanted to contact Colin Pinder and confront him. I wanted to know why he'd attacked my father with such violence – and why he'd deserted me, leaving me with the sole responsibility of bringing up his son, without contact or maintenance.

The people in the hostel made some phone calls to Liverpool and found rooms for us there, and then, on a sunny day in May, we travelled over on the boat. Liam, who was about five, was delighted to be going on a trip. His excitement reminded me of similar journeys my family and I had taken with my mother and how we'd believe we were heading off on an adventure. Bernard, of course, was still too young to understand what was happening.

Although I didn't know it at the time, I was on the verge of beginning a process that would shatter the false world that had imprisoned me since my father's murder.

Ten

Finding the Courage to Talk

We settled into our new surroundings. The rooms we were allocated in the refuge were spacious and we met some lovely families. Each woman had her own story of an abusive or unstable relationship, and everyone was just happy to have somewhere safe to settle. But despite the friendly, open atmosphere, I still couldn't sleep. When I did nod off I'd have my old nightmare. However, I enrolled the boys in national and nursery school and worked out a routine to take me through each day.

Over the next few weeks I became friendly with a woman called Pauline who worked in the refuge. She had been in a bad situation and had stayed at the hostel on a few occasions in the past. She'd great pluck and determination, and had undertaken to turn her life around. After returning to adult education, she now worked in the hostel, providing advice and comfort to women who'd been in violent relationships or had, for whatever reason, become homeless. She was one of the nicest and most sympathetic people I'd ever met. I felt safe in her company. She often brought in a video when she was on duty. A group of us would watch it together or she'd sit with us over a pot of tea and chat.

I didn't plan to tell her about what had happened to my father. But one night, the two of us were sitting together, discussing our lives. The other residents had gone to bed or were watching television. Pauline must have said something to trigger it but suddenly I had a lump in my throat and broke down in tears. When I recovered I found myself talking about the night of my father's murder. And once I'd started I couldn't stop. Everything poured out of me. I had to take a break many times to compose myself but she was very patient.

If she was horrified she showed no signs of it, and her calmness steadied me. Sometimes I was overcome by the horror of what I was telling her. For the first time in six years I was able to express myself. I wondered if she thought I was strung out on drugs or suffering from a mental disorder. I wouldn't have blamed her. She nodded, as if she understood, when I told her my mother had made me promise not to tell anyone about my father's death and how terrified I'd been to break that vow. She was an amazing listener. When the dawn came up and light streamed through the windows, I felt emptied out and exhausted, but lighter in my heart than I'd felt in years. I couldn't believe I'd plucked up the courage to tell the truth. For the first time in ages, I slept soundly for a few hours.

That morning I brought the boys to their schools and returned to the hostel. I was asked to go into the staff room where Pauline was waiting with other members of the staff. She asked for my permission to share my story with them and began to cry when she saw me. She asked me to repeat what I'd told her the previous night. I went through every detail again. When I finished, some of the women were also crying. They looked devastated but they put their arms around me and assured me that everything would be okay. Their solidarity gave me hope that my life had to change for the better. I understood that they would have to contact the police but I didn't grasp the full significance of this development until later. For the moment I felt only relief.

The next morning they called the police. A solicitor who would represent me arrived at the hostel where the interview would take place. The women's reassurances helped me to overcome my fear of going public and talking to the police.

When they arrived, Pauline smiled at me before I entered the room where I was to be interviewed. She pressed something into my hand. When I looked down I saw it was a prayer with a picture of Jesus on the cross. It was called 'The Cross in My Pocket'.

I carry a cross in my pocket,
A simple reminder to me
Of the fact that I am a Christian,
No matter where I may be.
This little cross is not magic
Nor is it a good luck charm.
It isn't meant to protect me
From every physical harm.
It's not for identification.
For all the world to see.
It's simply an understanding
Between my Saviour and me
When I put my hand in my pocket
To bring out a coin or key,
The cross is there to remind me
Of the price He paid for me.
It reminds me, too, to be thankful
For my blessings day by day,
And strive to serve Him better
In all that I do and say.
It's also a daily reminder
Of the peace and comfort I share
With all who know my Master
And give themselves to His care.
So, I carry a cross in my pocket,

Reminding no one but me
That Jesus Christ is Lord of my life,
If only I'll let Him be.

As I read the prayer, I felt the strength I needed to walk into the interview room flow into me. When I entered, a female detective in plain clothes, a policeman in uniform and my solicitor were seated behind a large table. The detective asked me to repeat my story.

Although she understood most of what I told her, the detective was confused over words like 'moulds', which was what I'd called the balustrades that had lain in the garden, one of which Colin Pinder had used to strike my father. She offered me a pen and paper and told me to draw a picture of a slash hook and a balustrade. I was questioned at length and went carefully over each detail. It was different from the intimate conversation I'd had with Pauline: the interview was formal and official. I was quite nervous, but the police did their best to put me at ease. My solicitor was also supportive, but my mind was racing ahead to my mother and how she would react when she discovered what I'd done. When the interview ended, the detective told me the police would be in touch with me. There was nothing I could do but wait.

The women in the refuge were fantastic. I'd been put on a waiting list for a house as soon as I arrived in Liverpool, and within a couple of weeks one came up. They said goodbye and told me they'd be thinking of me. If I needed anything I was to come back to them. I'll never forget their help and support.

Our new home was ideal for two small boys, with a front and back garden. But it was in a tough working-class area on the outskirts of the city. We settled in as best we could and I made it as comfortable I was able. Liam went to the local school and I enrolled Bernard in nursery school. As the weeks passed I waited for the police to make contact. When I heard nothing I became more and more jittery. I wondered if Colin and my mother had been taken in for questioning. I imagined them in handcuffs and my mind shied away from such an unbelievable image.

I called to Colin's family home to see if he'd been in contact with them. His mother was surprised to see me and didn't look particularly pleased. I was left standing on the doorstep and she pulled the door closed behind her. She was wary, clearly anxious for me to leave. Colin hadn't returned to Liverpool, she told me, and he was content with his life. I burst into tears. I knew the police could call to her house at any time. I told her that Colin had been involved in a crime. She demanded to know what he'd done. I could hardly bring myself to say the words but she waited, expressionless, until I finally told her. We didn't have much to say to each other after that and I could tell that she wanted me gone. I turned away and heard the door click behind me. Shaken, I took a bus back to the refuge where I had stayed, and was thankful once more for the support of the women who had first helped me tell my story.

Some weeks later a knock came to my door. Colin's brother and his wife were standing outside. I invited them in. The atmosphere was grim. They looked extremely worried and upset. Colin's brother asked why I'd made such an accusation. He wanted to know the full facts. I told them everything but they couldn't give me any information on Colin's whereabouts. I'd no way of knowing if they believed me but they seemed very troubled when they left.

It had been an upsetting encounter and I rang Philip in Ireland. We still kept in touch occasionally and it was good to hear a familiar voice. I told him how low I felt, though not why. He knew I was prone to depression and sudden bouts of weeping, and thought I was heading that way again. He asked if he should come over to stay for a few days, and I agreed.

Despite our differences, it was good to see him. When he was leaving he suggested that the boys and I should come for a holiday to Ireland. We could stay with him. I wasn't sure I wanted to become seriously involved with him again but I thought a short break from the unnerving wait for police contact could do no harm.

When I arrived in Ireland I told Philip the truth. Like everyone who heard the story, he was astonished and horrified. He was surprised that the UK police had not been back to me and said he would contact his own solicitor, who could advise me on how to proceed. We made an appointment to see him and he, in turn, contacted Detective Garda John Maunsell and Detective Garda Kevin Tunney. They were stationed in Dublin and came to Navan to interview me in Philip's house. I was nervous and apprehensive, but glad to see them. They did their best to put me at my ease and encouraged me to go through each stage of the murder and the aftermath.

They came back to the house a number of times to take further statements. John Maunsell recorded everything in his notes. When his hand became cramped from writing, he'd stop to shake his fingers, then start writing again. I accompanied them to hardware shops in the vicinity to point out the type of spanner and slash hook similar to those used in the murder. They gave me confidence that everything would be resolved and they promised to contact the local Gardaí in Granard, who would follow up on their investigations.

The following day the Gardaí from Granard arrived to Philip's house. They asked me to go with them in an unmarked car to the field in Coole to point out where my father had been killed. My mother, of course, was in Navan, oblivious to what was about to unfold around her.

Eleven

The Long Wait

It was November and the weather was bitterly cold. I stood outside the bedroom window and pointed out where my father had been standing when Colin first hit him. By now I was used to telling my story but it didn't make it any easier. Retelling everything at the scene was much worse. Images of my father lying on his hip and begging for mercy, his efforts to defend himself with the ladder, all the scenes of that horrendous night flashed before me. I walked around to the side of the house where he'd fallen and been struck by my mother. We went outside to the lane where he'd sought protection in the ditch. Finally, we walked through the field and I showed them where he'd been buried.

128

As I stood there in the biting cold, I wondered what I had set in train by going to the police. Everything was outside my control now and events would take their own course. But what if it wasn't the right course? Maybe the safer option would have been to remain quiet, and continue to bear the weight of my secret burden. But this feeling didn't last. The one thought that kept me going was the hope that the Gardaí would find evidence to support my story.

A team of forensic experts from Garda Headquarters in Dublin arrived in Coole to begin their investigations. The septic tank was emptied into a trench filled with plastic sheeting and the dig began. I prayed that they would find enough evidence to carry out a full-scale investigation. If they didn't, I'd be branded as either crazy or a vindictive liar. I was glad I'd met Detectives John Maunsell and Kevin Tunney first: they'd made it easy for me to tell the truth and they'd been supportive throughout the interviews. The Granard Gardaí were more formal in their dealings with me.

Within hours of the dig beginning, the story broke on the evening news. It was announced that an examination of our land was under way. Much to my relief, my name wasn't mentioned. My mother was still working in Navan as a child-minder and had no idea that I'd contacted the police. Half of me wanted to tell her face to face but the other half was terrified of confronting her. I could only imagine her shock as the news was broadcast and the media arrived in Coole to await the results.

I returned to Philip's house in Navan and began the agonising wait to hear the outcome. A few days after the dig had begun, Superintendent Liam Ward from Granard Garda Station knocked on the door and said, 'You'll be happy to know that we've had a result.' He added that they now knew I was telling the truth, that I was not mad and that I had not imagined what I'd reported to them.

I felt huge relief. They'd found some human remains, scraps of clothing, coins dated 1987 and earlier. The fabric was from the sleeve of a red jumper or cardigan; there was also a fragment from a white and green striped shirt, some heavy brown cloth, a piece of elasticated material and a label from a garment made of polyester and cotton with a nylon lining.

The forensics team took away five of the balustrades that were lying around the garden, a pitchfork, a jemmy, an iron bar, a shovel with no handle and a spade, along with briquettes they'd found in a plastic bag and two knives. In the sludge from the septic tank they found a watch without its strap, an iron bar and some animal bones.

The grave where my dad had been buried measured six feet by four and was eighteen inches deep. As well as the coins and fabric, the forensics team had found briquettes, timber and, most upsetting of all, a jaw bone with four teeth that looked human. Other bones were from a human arm and a hand that showed it had been severed.

By now my mother knew she was under suspicion but she still had no confirmation of who was responsible for alerting the Gardaí. I lay low at Philip's house and made no contact.

She was arrested on 10 November 1993, as she was getting out of her car in Townspark, and driven to Mullingar Garda Station. She was questioned there for two days. We waited anxiously for news but heard nothing. It was a difficult time for my brothers. For six years they'd believed their father didn't love them. Their mother had told them he was a bad father who'd deserted them. When they had never received a letter or a phone call from him, they had believed she was right and that he'd abandoned us. Now they didn't know what to think. I kept praying that when they heard it was their sister who had gone to the guards, they would understand why I'd done it.

On the second day of my mother's arrest, she made a statement admitting she had played a part in the murder of my father. She claimed she'd struck him only once and that Colin Pinder was the real killer. She was released and returned to her home in Navan. A few days later she was driven by the Gardaí to Coole and asked to point out where the murder had taken place.

In December, Detectives Kevin Tunney and John Maunsell travelled to Yorkshire to interview Colin

Pinder. Colin was in a relationship with a different woman and they were living in West Yorkshire. From the day he'd walked away from Coole he'd had no contact with our son – he hadn't sent him so much as a birthday or a Christmas card. He had been truly determined to banish the past, but now it was catching up with him. At the time, we weren't told what he said to the guards during that interview. Indeed, it would be many years before it was revealed.

I suspect my mother hoped that Colin Pinder would be charged with the murder and that she would walk free. She still didn't know why the Gardaí had started the investigation and called to see me after her release. I made her tea and listened as she complained about the treatment she'd received at the Garda station. She didn't trust the guards, apart from the female officer to whom she'd made her statement. She felt she'd been treated in a degrading way, with no privacy when she wanted to use the toilet or wash herself, and she hadn't been allowed a cigarette when she needed one.

As she continued talking, giving a blow-by-blow account of her experience, wondering aloud why the guards had been alerted, I felt the knot tighten in my stomach. I finally blurted out the truth. I explained, as best I could, my reasons for going to the police – the burden of a guilty secret that I was no longer able to bear.

Much to my surprise, she didn't react as I'd expected. I could see she was startled but she didn't fly into a rage. Instead she became very quiet. A short while later, remarkably, she said, 'I understand why you did it.'

But the atmosphere remained tense. She left soon afterwards. A few days later I visited her at her house. It was early in the morning but she was up and dressed. She said, 'I'm glad you came. I feel stronger now that you're here.' It was a rare moment of closeness. Strange that it should come from such bitter circumstances.

Some time after that, the official Garda dig ended. I decided to stay in Ireland and give my relationship with Philip another chance. I found myself clinging to him for moral support but, as usual, it was an up-and-down relationship, and my mother's regular visits to the bungalow didn't help matters. Her calm when she'd returned from the Garda interrogation had changed to fury. She was on edge all the time waiting for news. On many occasions she'd go into a rant and accuse me of destroying her life. She'd remind me that she could be facing time in Mountjoy Jail. If that happened, the boys would lose their mother and I'd be responsible for breaking up our family. At other times, she'd be friendly and chatty, as if nothing had happened between us. These occasions were almost worse: I'd be on tenterhooks, waiting for her mood to change and all hell to break loose.

Our already dysfunctional home was falling further apart. Nothing would ever be the same again. The older boys were working now but the publicity that followed the discovery of our father's remains was difficult for them. They also had to come to terms with the truth. For good or bad, I had let them believe their father was in Holland and I'd no way of knowing how they felt about me.

As the months passed and we heard nothing, our mother signed up for educational courses and began working with the Alzheimer's Association, driving patients to and from their homes. I was busy, too, working in a takeaway in Navan. Philip would mind Liam and Bernard while I was on duty. When I had managed to save enough money, I took out a loan from the Credit Union so that work could begin on my own house. I had an extension built at the back, a new roof, a bathroom and a toilet. I painted it, and Robert, a friend from Navan, helped me to install the fireplace. He was about seven years younger than me but he was good company and fun to have around. He'd a great way with the boys and they loved it when he called.

Philip had moved out of his bungalow and we lived together in my new house. But our relationship remained difficult and we decided, once again, to go our separate ways. My mother was in another relationship. She and her partner were frequent visitors, and she often demanded my bedroom for their overnight stays. Nothing, it seemed, ever changed when it came to Vera and me.

Robert called regularly with his friends. We'd have a few beers and a laugh. They were young and carefree and I enjoyed their company. It was an opportunity to catch up on the fun I'd missed in my teens. I could forget about being a mother of two small children and just relax for a change, make up for lost opportunities. I was twenty-nine and, when I thought back, it was hard to remember a time when I wasn't weighed down with depression or in a fug of anti-depressants. That brief spell of happiness when Colin had proposed to me seemed to belong to someone else's life.

In March 1995 I discovered I was pregnant again. Robert and I had only been together a couple of times – and the result of our brief, carefree relationship came as a shock to both of us. He was kind and considerate but he was too young to settle down and cope with the responsibility of a baby. Even if he had been older I wasn't prepared to settle down with him. I was alone again, facing the consequences of my own recklessness. I'd made my bed, as the older people used to say, and now I had to lie in it on my own.

Bernard would be five when the next baby arrived. On this occasion, thankfully, I went through none of the bleak depression I'd endured with my last pregnancy. Philip was a good support – I don't know how he felt about the situation with Robert but he was never judgemental and I could always rely on him in a crisis.

In the meantime my mother and her partner wanted to have their own space. As the boys were still living in Townspark, they left them in the house, intending to rent a place for themselves elsewhere. While they were waiting for something to become available, she arrived to my house one day and asked if they could stay with me for the time being. She said they would use my bedroom and that I could manage quite well in the smaller room. I was halfway through my pregnancy and suffering from backache but, meekly, I gave in. It was a crazy situation. We were both waiting for the results of the Garda investigation to come through yet there we were, living cheek by jowl with each other in my small house. Thankfully, it wasn't long before they moved into their own place, and I could breathe normally again.

I wanted to manage my pregnancy without my mother's help. A neighbour, who was also a friend, promised to take care of Liam and Bernard when the time came to go to the hospital. Christmas was coming and I was busy preparing the house for Santa. The decorations were up, the lights twinkling and the stockings filled when I woke early on Christmas morning. The boys were still sleeping but the new arrival wasn't hanging around. Eight years previously on the Christmas Eve, Liam had made his appearance and I couldn't believe the timing of this new arrival.

It was a freezing, blustery Christmas morning with a sprinkling of snow. I called to my friend's house and rang the doorbell. The house was in darkness. When there was no answer, I began to panic. I returned to the house and woke the boys. I explained that there was no time to look at what Santa had brought. Another Christmas present, a little sister or brother, was on its way. There was only one thing to do. I walked them both to my mother's house, which wasn't that far away, and told her what was happening. She came back to my house with the children and her partner, and I rang Philip. He drove around and whisked me into Our Lady of Lourdes Hospital in Drogheda.

I gave birth to Clare, a beautiful little girl, and cried with happiness when she was placed in my arms. She had downy blonde hair and was absolutely gorgeous. I'd always wanted a little sister, and now I had my own baby girl. I was allowed home later that evening so I got to spend some precious Christmas time with my boys.

I still remember how happy I was and how excited the boys were when they saw their special Christmas present for the first time. My mother, who always responded to small babies, said she was the most beautiful baby she'd ever seen. It was rare for her to be in such good spirits and I believe she genuinely loved my daughter.

It was hard to manage with three young children and no back-up support. Philip, who had bought a house close by, suggested that we move in with him again. I rented my own house and was living with him when, in October 1996, the shocking news of the investigation results finally came – and in a most bizarre way.

My mother had received a letter from the guards,

which had been delivered to her solicitor. She wasted no time in arriving at our doorstep with the news. The message was unambiguous: 'I confirm that the Garda investigation into this case has concluded and no prosecution will take place.'

'You thought you'd got me,' she said, over and over, as she waved the letter in the air.

I was speechless. My mother was telling me that she was a free woman, that no prosecution was to be taken against her. It was simply unbelievable. She had *admitted* to Gardaí that she had a part in my father's murder. They had unearthed teeth and bone fragments, and even a piece of my father's shirt on the site. Yet, for whatever reasons, they'd exonerated the people responsible and I'd failed to get justice for my dad. I'd not only let him down, but caused huge distress to my brothers.

I had trusted the Gardaí, and it had been misplaced. Now I had to cope with the fallout from bringing the attention of the Gardaí and the media to our family. I felt sick with disappointment and shame. I agonised over why I'd opened my mouth in the first place. And now, as the media attention died away, Vera McGrath believed she was untouchable.

Twelve

The Aftermath

I felt betrayed by the system. The people who had killed my father were free to carry on their lives as if nothing had happened. Three years of waiting had been reduced to one curt, official line: 'I confirm that the Garda investigation into this case has concluded and no prosecution will take place.' Unbelievable as it seemed, given all the evidence that had been uncovered, the decision had been made and I was back to square one. And that old black dog of depression once more held me within its jaws.

I tried to fight it. My three children were dependent on me. All I wanted to do was give them the love and attention they deserved. In an effort to lift my mood I'd started a fitness regime. Every evening, once the children were settled, I'd do a workout. But I knew enough about depression to recognise the danger signs. I was taking too many tablets, slowing down, letting myself go again. I gave myself pep talks but my self-loathing, never far below the surface, was rising. So, too, were the nightmares. Now that a decision had been made by the state not to take action, my dreams took on a more terrifying intensity.

My mother, on the other hand, had never been in better form. She'd call to the house and regale us with stories of her love life. I was sick listening to the same intimate details being repeated, sick of her need to dominate and be the centre of attention, negative or positive. I'd been down the same road too often and I wanted off it but I didn't know which way to turn. I had a history of failed relationships, unplanned pregnancies and chronic depression. And now my effort to do the one decent thing I could in my life – achieve justice for my murdered father – had failed.

One particular evening my mother dropped by. My mind switched off as she carried on with her usual chatter. I saw her lips moving but I no longer had any idea what she was saying to Philip. All I knew was I couldn't go on any longer. I had no fight left. Once my decision was made a feeling of utter calm came over me.

I can't remember if it was that evening or the

following evening that I took action. I made tea for the children and put them to bed. I did my exercise routine and took a shower. I sat down and wrote a letter to my children. I told them I loved them dearly and asked them never to forget me. Then I wrote a second letter outlining everything that had happened the night my father died. I was calm and resolute as I swallowed the tablets. It was as if a radio that had been crackling with white noise for too long in my mind had been switched off and all that remained was a peaceful silence.

The next thing I remember is waking up in the bedroom. My mother was leaning over me. She sounded frantic, shaking me and demanding to know what I'd taken. Over the next few days I was walked up and down the room, plunged into baths of cold water, forced to throw up and brought to the beaches in Laytown and Bettystown to walk off the effects in the fresh air. This is what I've been told by members of my family but I have no memory of that time.

Looking back, it seems inconceivable that I could have tried to take my life when I had a young family. But I can't pretend it was a cry for help. I was going on a journey and I'd no intention of coming back. In the aftermath, I thought it would be impossible to continue living but, somehow, I did. I was ashamed of my actions, especially when I looked into the innocent faces of my children. I struggled on, placed one foot in front of the other, and tried to get the psychiatric help I needed. I remember attending one psychiatrist who was amazed that I was alive. His advice at the end of the session was to take Prozac and pray.

I continued to let my house on St Patrick's Terrace and moved with my children and Philip to nearby Lanesboro in Roscommon and, eventually, spent some time in the psychiatric unit in Roscommon County Hospital. I came out of there feeling a lot stronger and determined to rebuild my life.

Ever since the DPP had announced its decision not to prosecute, I'd been determined to claim my father's few remains, which had been found on the murder site, and lay what was left of him with dignity in consecrated ground. Then, perhaps, he would finally be at rest. My mother was opposed to the idea of a funeral and we argued fiercely about it. I was a thorn in her side, the one person who refused to let the past go. But I was determined that my father would have a grave and an inscription that acknowledged his existence on this earth.

I contacted Denis Naughten, a Fine Gael TD, and told him about my difficulties getting back my father's remains from the Gardaí. During Dáil QuestionTime he raised my query about when my father's remains would be returned to his family. A local social worker was also very supportive and helped me to write to the appropriate authorities. Eventually, in June 1998, our efforts paid off. The teeth and bones that had been unearthed were handed over to the undertaker by a plain-clothes guard in the morgue in Mullingar. They had been placed in a bucket and I was appalled by the callous indifference of the Gardaí, considering the circumstances of my father's death. But the undertaker treated his remains with respect. They were placed in a velvet bag and laid in the coffin. I put in a letter, with some religious medals, roses and a poem from my sons. Liam rode in the front seat of the hearse. I followed in my own car, with Bernard and Clare, and played my father's favourite songs on the car stereo as we drove to Coole.

A funeral mass was celebrated in Coole Church and the building was packed. I was delighted that so many of our old neighbours and friends came. Liam and I did a reading. For once I felt I was doing something to make my father proud and I was glad that my son had a chance to say goodbye to the grandfather he had never known.

My father was buried in Whitehall Cemetery, and afterwards we all went to the Castlepollard Arms. Brian McGrath was getting the send-off he deserved in the traditional Irish style. I felt at peace when I returned to my home that evening. If there was a heaven, then his spirit was finally there, and I was happy for him.

I had a longing to live in the country and set about finding a suitable house. My relationship with Philip, though up and down, was back on again and I drove around Roscommon and finally found the perfect place. It was an old farmhouse in a lovely setting and we moved in shortly afterwards.

I found work as a care assistant with the Irish Wheelchair Association, at Cuisle Holiday Centre, on the site of Donamon Castle. The holiday centre caters for adults and children with or without disabilities. I loved working with the guests, helping them with their wheelchairs, walking with them through the wonderful gardens and offering any assistance I could to make their stay as enjoyable as possible. I also made friends with the staff and the supervisors.

Once again my relationship with Philip came to an end. He returned to Navan and I continued living in Roscommon. I became involved with a mental health self-help group, Grow, aimed at supporting people with emotional difficulties. It works on recovery and personal growth, and we met once a week. It was great to talk with people I could trust and who understood the struggle involved in coping with depression and low self-esteem.

This brief good spell wasn't to last though. All staff at the holiday centre were told that they would need Garda clearance if they were to continue providing care for the residents. In light of the revelations over sex abuse in state-run institutions, regulations were being tightened up in every area where services were provided for children and vulnerable adults. I filled out the necessary documentation, along with the rest of the staff, and, gradually, other people's clearance began to come through. I waited for mine to arrive and thought nothing when at first it seemed to be delayed. I figured the Gardaí were just dealing with a backlog. But as time passed my supervisor began to worry on my behalf. I made enquiries but to no avail. Finally, I was the only staff member who had not received the necessary clearance.

Reluctantly, my supervisor was forced to deal with the situation. Under new regulations, I could no longer work with the residents as a carer at Cuisle. I was devastated. There could be only one reason why my clearance had not been granted. I'd reported a crime and a question mark was now hanging over my head. I was offered alternative work in the kitchens at Cuisle but I was too upset and humiliated to accept it. Ironically, my mother, who had held down a number of jobs, including driving sick people around in a bus, had been cleared in 1997 – after she had confessed to being involved in my father's murder. And she was still collecting her Deserted Wives' Allowance.

With all that had happened, and the knowledge that I was now excluded from jobs involving children and vulnerable adults, I decided to leave Ireland. On the advice of a friend who was living and working in Wales, I decided to try my luck in Cardiff. Liam, who was almost a teenager and had started secondary school, was dead set against the move. He was starting to rebel and, though I understood his behaviour – God knows, he'd put up with a lot of upheaval over the years – it didn't make it any easier to handle.

I drove to Navan to tell my family what I intended

to do. Liam got on well with his uncles and he wanted to stay in Navan, where he also had friends. My mother offered to look after him until I'd found a place to settle down. Her relationship with her grandchildren was solid, and Liam seemed content to remain with her, but I hated leaving him behind. However, he was as headstrong in wanting to stay as I was determined to leave. I took Bernard and Clare with me and we headed for Wales.

Thirteen

The Intruder

My friend Jerome was living in Cardiff. He'd arranged accommodation for us in a hostel for the homeless, run by *The Big Issue*. After we had settled in and I'd organised school and crèche for the children, I started selling *The Big Issue* magazine on the streets. To my surprise, it turned out to be a very positive experience. I discovered I was good at selling and earned myself a prime pitch outside a River Island shop in the centre of Cardiff. I found the public courteous and kind, often buying coffee or soup for me. Sometimes, if they didn't want to buy a magazine, they'd press money into my hand, especially around Christmas time when it could be as much as a five-pound note. They'd often stop to chat, which meant a lot to me. I was no longer an invisible nobody in the middle of this busy city. My dignity was being restored to me. Some of the vendors had problems with drugs or alcohol, and if there was a downside of the job, it was the bullying that sometimes took place to move me on from a prime pitch.

The Big Issue organisation is run on the basis that people in difficult situations need a hand *up*, not a hand*out* – and the sellers had to follow certain regulations. We had to be on time for work and keep to our agreed pitches. We were not allowed bring our children to work and I put in my hours around the children's school and crèche times. The staff at the hostel were practical and supportive. We were supposed to stay out during the day but they stretched the rules and provided me with a room where I could bring the kids and make tea and sandwiches for them. If I was short of money and needed to do extra hours when they were off school or on holidays, I'd bring them to the library where activities were arranged or I'd stretch to a McDonald's and work outside while keeping an eye on them. Within a short while, *The Big Issue* staff provided me with a terraced house on Emerald Street in Cardiff. Just as I was getting settled my mother rang. She told me to come home and collect Liam. She had moved back into the family home in Coole and she wanted time alone with her partner. Liam still wasn't happy about moving to Wales but now he had no choice. I headed back home and we returned to Cardiff together. I continued selling *The Big Issue* and we managed as best we could. When I had to work overtime to make ends meet, Liam would look after the younger children. It wasn't an ideal situation but we managed to get by.

Around this time I made one special friend I'll always remember. David, a transsexual, was one of the kindest, most gentle people I'd ever met. He wrote poetry and some of it was published in *The Big Issue* to his delight. We'd often have a cup of coffee together when I'd take a break from selling and discuss our strange, complicated lives. He was jeered at and abused by some people for dressing in women's clothes. He coped as best he could and found great solace in his poetry, and also from the work he did in *The Big Issue* office.

Jerome called regularly to the house to see us. I enjoyed his company until our friendship took a dramatic turn for the worse and an incident occurred that would have far-reaching effects on me and my children. One evening he dropped into my house with another man, whom he introduced as Theo. I took an instant dislike to Theo. From his fidgety movements and the restless way he kept looking around, I figured he had a drug problem and was relieved when they left the house. On a few occasions afterwards I saw Jerome and Theo together on the street but Theo never came back with Jerome to visit me. I was always courteous when we met but kept a polite distance from him.

One day, when Jerome was in the house, I answered a knock on the door. Theo was standing outside. He asked to speak to Jerome. It was urgent, he said, so I allowed him in. They were talking to each other for a while when an argument broke out. Suddenly, they were shouting at each other. The children were in the house and I was worried a fight would start. My fears were justified. A few minutes later there were fisticuffs. I yelled at them to get out but they paid no heed. Theo was stronger than Jerome and obviously high on drugs. He grabbed Jerome, shoved him to the front door and flung him out into the street. By now I was in a barely controlled panic, trying to protect the kids from what was happening.

Next thing, Theo pulled a knife and held it to my throat. He roared at me to keep my mouth shut, to obey his orders and not dare to alert anyone. He threatened to rape me in front of the children if I didn't do as I was told. He warned me not to move as he withdrew the knife and set about locking the doors, front and back. He grabbed Bernard, locked him in his bedroom, ordered him to do sit-ups and not to make a sound. I was too frightened to unlock the door in case he hurt Bernard, or worse. I tried talking Theo down but he wouldn't listen. I'd no idea what drugs he was on, only that he was in the grip of a manic rage, off his head. I did my best to keep calm and bided my time until, with the help of God, we could escape.

At one stage Theo put on the stereo at full volume, a Pink Floyd album. He told me to get a pen and paper and write down the lyrics. I tried, but I'd always had difficulties with writing and, besides, my hand was shaking so much it was impossible to keep up with the words. Then he'd scream at me or hit me and call me stupid. I kept praying that Jerome had gone to the police but time passed and there was no sign of help.

Theo's mood was becoming more and more vicious. He found a hammer and banged it off the wall. He ordered food, and as I made the sandwiches, he stood behind me with the knife, threatening me if I made a false move. I begged him to put the knife away for the children's sake. Clare remained very quiet and subdued throughout. I only hoped she was too young to understand the danger we were in. I kept whispering to her, reassuring her that everything was going to be all right.

Liam was trying to think of an escape plan but Theo dictated every move we made. Sometimes he'd put the knife into his pocket but I knew he'd pull it out again at the slightest provocation. It's hard to know how long this ordeal lasted. Minutes passed like hours. Somehow, we got through the night. The children were so exhausted they eventually fell asleep.

Next day we were out of food. Theo was coming down from his high and was starving. I suggested that

Liam go to the local chipper at the top of the street. As I handed him the money, I whispered that he was to tell the police. He had already decided on the same plan, and as soon as he was free, he ran directly to the nearest police station.

About twenty minutes later the police kicked in the door. A helicopter flew low over the roof. Theo gave in without a fight. He still had the knife and was disarmed, then handcuffed. I was so proud of Liam that day – proud of all my children for how they'd handled such a traumatic ordeal. They'd come through it without antagonising the crazed man, which would only have made a dire situation worse. They had helped us all to stay alive. After Theo was taken off in a squad car I gathered the children close to me, kissed them and told them how much I loved them.

I gave my statement to the police, and alternative accommodation was arranged for us in a hostel far away from Cardiff – we were too afraid to stay in the house. It was in a remote part of the country and we stayed there until we felt strong enough to move on.

Our attacker was committed to a psychiatric hospital. As for Jerome, I've not seen him since that day.

Fourteen

Heartbreaking Decisions

Afterwards, understandably, Clare was afraid to let me out of her sight. Liam was also profoundly upset. But I felt most concerned for Bernard, who'd been kept isolated without any idea of what was taking place downstairs. As for me, I lived in a state of constant terror. I'd jump out of my skin if a piece of paper blew past me.

We spent a few weeks in the Welsh hostel before I decided to move to Cambridge. I'd heard it was a lovely city and hoped it might be a quiet place to bring up the children. I found accommodation in a council flat and we settled in quickly. The children started at a new school but life was far from smooth. I'd been holding my family together by a thread and I didn't know how much longer I could go on. My depression was severe and I was verging on a nervous breakdown. I knew that I needed psychiatric care but was worried about who would take care of the children if I was taken into hospital.

My relationship with the boys was becoming increasingly difficult. I felt guilty and inadequate as a mother. I wanted to provide my children with a stable environment and the security they needed, but no matter what I did, it never seemed to work out. Loving them was not enough. They needed so much more.

I was regularly reduced to tears as I begged my sons to do as I asked them. Any authority I'd had over them seemed gone, as was my energy for the fight. They lacked a strong father figure in their lives and needed one. They'd had an unsettled upbringing, and, on top of everything, their home, which should have been a safe refuge, had been invaded by a drug-crazed madman. I'd failed to protect my family. No wonder they were angry. And no wonder I, being the closest to them, was the focus of that anger.

As a family we were desperately in need of counselling. I didn't have the money to pay for private sessions so I asked Social Services for help but none was forthcoming. As always, I stuck to my policy of putting one foot in front of the other, living one day at a time.

I'd no desire to return home and listen to my mother telling me I was incapable of coping.

There was a family in the flat downstairs from us who clearly had problems. I'd hear loud arguments and music playing at all hours. I didn't want Liam mixing with them and I tried to find somewhere else for us to live. Social Services didn't want to know. As far as they were concerned, we had perfectly adequate accommodation.

I told the boys I was leaving to find a new place for us to live but they refused to come with me. We argued; they resisted. Something snapped inside me. The constant fighting, screaming and tears had defeated me. The same calm came over me as when I had tried to take my life, but this time I knew that suicide was not the answer. I loved my children with all my heart but I understood I was no longer capable of giving them the support and care they needed. It was in these circumstances that I made the hardest decision of my life.

I left them in the flat and went to the police. I told them that my two boys were alone at home and I could no longer care for them. I asked for Social Services to take them into foster care.

The police took immediate action and Social Services responded, as I'd hoped they would. My boys were taken under their wing but they allowed me to keep Clare.

I was torn apart over my decision and thought of

my boys night and day. But it was some weeks before I saw them. Outwardly they seemed settled and content with the new arrangement, though I've no idea what was going on in their young minds. Yet I was grateful that they were being cared for properly, well fed and clothed, with a caring family unit around them. It was an awful situation but I knew it was the only option at the time. The social workers told me that as soon as I felt I could manage the boys again I could get in touch with them.

After that I saw them on a number of occasions. I was still in crisis, but Clare was a quiet, lovable child and we were getting by. The boys were living within the local area and I was walking the streets, worried that I might bump into them, and ashamed that I still couldn't take them back. Would they resent the fact that I'd kept Clare? Would they believe I loved her more? I loved all of my children equally, but life was complicated and I knew it would be hard for them to understand.

I moved with Clare to Bath and tried to get my life back on track. I'd started over so many times by now that I'd lost count. I'd survived somehow. But this time was different: the council could not provide us with any accommodation and my only option was a homeless shelter. But when I arrived I discovered that it would only take in adults for the night. For the first time in my life I ended up on the streets, with my small daughter beside me. The shelter provided me with sleeping bags and I'd seek out places during the day where it would be safe to sleep that night.

I hit rock bottom in Bath and it was a horrifying existence. We had to beg for food, and rely on handouts of blankets, tea and coffee. I lived in dread that something bad would happen to Clare. The shock of being homeless hit hard. When you haven't got a stable family background, and are reliant on medication for depression, you can be easy pickings for unscrupulous or crazy people. We'd survived that attack in Wales but it must have had a traumatic effect on my children.

It had certainly affected me. I sensed danger around every corner. The nightmares of old had returned, only this time I was waking up without my two boys and staring into the pitch black of an empty street, my young daughter huddled into me. Some nights we slept in public toilets along the seafront, or in shop doorways, under archways or on a park bench huddled together to keep warm. The noise from traffic was constant. Occasionally we had to move on quickly if a fight broke out, or if alcoholics or drug addicts insisted on taking our space. But, thankfully – luckily – we came safely through this ordeal without anything bad happening to us. It must have been scary for Clare and I'd try to make it as bearable as possible for her.

During the day we'd go to the swimming pool and use the showers. If this wasn't possible, we washed in public toilets. But it's impossible to keep clean when you're on the streets night and day. Later, the council provided us with a room in a B&B on the outskirts of the city. But the same problem existed of how to pass the time with a small child. It was exhausting walking around all day trying to find things to do. We passed time in libraries and churches, wandered around the shops, ate in cafés and at McDonald's. But it was a dangerous lifestyle and it couldn't continue. Clare was only five years old and I was responsible for her safety. If it hadn't been for her, and my determination to get my boys back, I would not have thought twice about ending it all. And this time I'd have made sure to do it properly.

I dreaded having to admit defeat, but I knew I had to return to the only person who understood why I was in such a mess. My mother and I had an impossible relationship, but we understood each other. It was this knowledge that kept drawing me back to her. I felt like a prisoner of my own past. We travelled back to Ireland, back to Coole, back to all I'd left behind.

I arrived home to Coole and told Vera what had happened. She reacted as I'd expected. When I was a child she'd told me many times that I was useless and stupid so this was nothing new. When I confessed that the past was still tormenting me, she ordered me to cop on and pull myself together. She offered to take care of Clare for me and insisted I return to England and sort myself out. Sorting myself out didn't seem to be such an issue for her. As for me, I didn't know where to begin. I could barely pull myself through each day. I wasn't eating properly. I looked like a wreck, unwashed, my hair in tangles, dependent on Valium and antidepressants. Anyone looking at me would have thought I was on heroin or mentally ill. And I *was* mentally ill. I just didn't realise how seriously so.

She said that once I'd settled in and found myself a job, I could bring Clare over to join me, and get the boys back. It shows the fantasy world we both occupied. What I needed was psychiatric care and counselling. In an ideal world that might have been possible but my world was far from ideal. I said goodbye to Clare and told her I'd be back soon, then returned to Bath.

I got in touch with *The Big Issue* and was given a pitch to sell the magazine. But I'd none of the energy or enthusiasm that had kept me going in Wales. Without Clare I was now eligible to sleep in the homeless shelter. It was located in a basement, and a case of first come first served every night. Sometimes the beds would be taken before I reached the top of the queue. I heard from one of *The Big Issue* vendors that there might be accommodation with a group of new-age travellers in a town called Radstock, in Somerset, just a few miles outside Bath. I made my way there and was offered a small caravan. I met families with children who had opted for an alternative lifestyle, musicians passing through, people who had simply dropped out of society, and those who, like myself, were trying a find a way back in. I lived for a short while within this new community but there were some serious heroin users there and this created tension within it. It wasn't the safest place to live or an option for Clare and the boys, if I managed to get them all together again.

I left Radstock and slept in a car for a few nights. Sometimes luck came my way. I'll never forget the generosity of a woman who stopped to buy a *Big Issue* from me. She asked me about myself and ended up inviting me back to her house for the night. I had a bath and a bed, and I shared her evening meal. Perhaps she was lonely. She lived alone but she did not tell me much about her life. Instead she let me talk and demanded nothing in return. When I was leaving she gave me a mobile phone as a present. Such encounters were important to my dignity, what little of it I still had.

I worked hard at selling *The Big Issue* and earned enough to travel back to Cambridge to see my two sons. I bought scooters for them – they were all the rage at the time. I met Liam and Bernard in the company of a social worker. The boys were doing fine and appeared to be content in their new home. I don't know what they thought of the state I was obviously in. I was also conscious of the social worker and ashamed that my life should have come to this.

Out of the blue, while I was in Cambridge I met David, the transsexual I'd befriended in Cardiff. He was now working in *The Big Issue* office and saving to go to London to have a total sex change operation. In Cardiff he was always well dressed and had kept himself in good nick but now I noticed a big change in him. He looked down-at-heel and weary, and was clearly finding life more difficult. In the end, it all proved too much for him. I was grief-stricken when I heard he'd committed suicide in the Cambridge hostel where he was staying. David was a lost soul and, heartbroken at his decision to take his life, I identified with his plight.

In the end, I admitted defeat and returned home. My mother was still working in Navan and she had enrolled Clare in a local school there. They'd travel from Coole each morning, which meant an early start to Clare's day. She had been instructed to call her grandmother Sara, as her other grandchildren had done, never 'Nana' or 'Granny'. Vera was still a very attractive woman, who took great care of her appearance. And if I'd been cast as the ugly duckling to her swan, neither of us ever failed to live up to expectations. While she could keep up appearances, no matter what the situation, I always fell foul of them, unable to pretend to the world that my life was other than it was: a chaotic mess.

Clare had been unhappy while I was away. My mother had been cross with her, impatient and insulting. When I challenged her about this, she called Clare a liar. As I listened to her undermining Clare and saw my daughter's unhappiness grow, I was determined that she would not suffer the childhood I'd endured. But to make this happen, I needed to get well again. I kept putting off the inevitable, but I knew I couldn't hold out much longer without psychiatric care.

Soon the UK social workers decided to send the boys home to Ireland to arranged foster care. I was living with Clare in my mother's other house in Navan and I was on my last legs. I sat down with Clare and asked her if she would like to go and stay with her brothers for a little break. She agreed that she was missing them and would love to see them. It was a relief to hear her say that. I didn't know how to explain to a little girl that her mammy was too sick to cope with her and life in general.

Once again I met with social workers and explained my circumstances. It was agreed that Clare would be better off in a safer and more stable environment. I asked if they could put her with her brothers until I got better. I didn't know then that the boys had been placed with separate families or that Clare would be placed with a family on her own. But the decision was out of my control. I left her in the care of social workers in Brews Hill, Navan. I was devastated but I knew it was the best thing.

When I returned home, all my suppressed rage at my mother came to the surface. Although I blamed myself for my problems, deep down I blamed her too. In my mind, she was at the root of them, right back to my childhood. If I'd had any kind of motherly love, some affirmation that I was not a bad person, things might have been so different.

'I hope you're satisfied now,' I yelled at her when I told her the decision I'd made but, as usual, my anger went over her head.

The social workers arranged for me to see Clare regularly. Many of our meetings took place at the health centre in Dunshaughlin. They were hard on both of us. We would play with the toys in the room and she would tell me how she was getting on with her foster family. She seemed happy, but although this was a relief, I was distraught because I wanted her to be happy with me.

She loved certain songs, like an old one called 'I've Got A Lovely Bunch Of Coconuts'. She would dance around the room, singing it to her heart's content. Her other favourite was 'I'm A Survivor' by Destiny's Child.

When it came time to go she would wrap her arms and legs around me, crying for me to take her home. It was devastating. All I wanted in life was to be well enough to set up a stable home for my children. But I knew that if I tried I'd be at rock bottom again within weeks. After leaving Clare I'd walk the streets all day, wishing I could go back and take her home with me. Some of the social workers were nice and went out of their way to help, but others were less sympathetic and I felt judged for abandoning my children. Having felt abandoned for most of my own life, I couldn't bear to think that my children would grow up feeling like that.

Eventually the visits with Clare became too much to bear. It was breaking my heart to have to walk away each time. I knew that it couldn't be good for her either. I decided to stop them until I was able to take her home with me for good. One day, in 2001, I made my last visit to the health centre. I'd bought the CD of 'I'm A Survivor' along with a little portable CD player. I wrote Clare a note telling her I would always love her and left it with the gifts. I cried all the way back to my mother's house in Townspark – my place of warped refuge whenever my life became unbearable.

I hardly ever drink, even in the worst of times, but that day, after I left the Social Services centre, I stopped off at the off-licence and bought a large bottle of vodka.

My mother, who still kept the house in Coole, was just leaving to drive there. She listened briefly to what I had to tell her about Clare, then departed. The house was empty and silent. I looked back over my life, the years that had gone by in a haze, the blanked-out memories, the overdose. I tried to remember my children as babies – their first teeth, their first time crawling, walking, their first words – but it was all a blur to me. Good mothers didn't forget those important events. Good mothers didn't fail to protect their children. I felt riddled with guilt. As a mother, it's the worst feeling in the world to have to admit you can't cope with your children – in effect that you have failed them.

I opened the bottle, poured a glass and began to drink. I poured and drank every drop. Then I closed and locked the door, turned on the gas and opened the oven door. I sat on a chair and prayed that God would take me quickly.

I've no idea how much time passed before I was discovered. A neighbour had smelt the gas and called an ambulance.

I regained consciousness in hospital and, once stabilised, was soon admitted to a small psychiatric unit in Navan, then transferred to St Brigid's Psychiatric Hospital in Ardee. This was a total breakdown and I honestly believed there was no way back. I'd no interest in eating; neither did I know or care if it was night or day. Various drug therapies were tried but none of them made any difference to my state. My mind was overactive, spinning out of control. I could feel physical pain in my body from the pressure of my mind. In desperation I agreed to undergo electroconvulsive therapy. I wanted to come back to life, to care about what happened to me, to plan for my future. I knew the risks associated with the treatment, one of them being a degree of memory loss. Did I really want to remember, I wondered, as I thought over my options. Looking back never gave me any comfort. I was informed that it could be more effective than the use of drugs to treat severe and chronic depression. In the past it had been a brutal method of treating mental disorders but I was assured that muscle relaxants and various anaesthetics would be used while it was being applied; they would make it much easier to endure.

An injection was administered before the shock treatment and for a few seconds my mind emptied. That sensation was wonderful. My mind was a blank canvas, with no memories of my father's head burning on a pitchfork, no memories of my children in care, no memories of a mother who despised me. For those few minutes I was free. But it didn't last. Once the relaxants wore off, the obsessive thoughts pushed their way back into my mind and I was back on the same old merry-go-round. Eventually I was discharged, with a cocktail of tablets and a sense that nothing had really changed.

My mother was relieved that I was out of hospital, although she'd never once visited me during my stay. Against my better judgement, and in a vain effort to bring my family back together, I rented a flat in Mullingar. It was small with bad lighting but all I could afford on my social welfare allowance. I rang Social Services to tell them I was ready to look after my children again. A social worker examined the flat and asked lots of questions about my situation. She said they'd make a decision when they'd found out about the local schools and decided if the flat was suitable. We both knew what the outcome would be – but I kept hoping it would be favourable. I knew deep down I still wasn't well enough to cope with them on my own: it was loneliness that was driving me to try to reunite my children. As I suspected, the social worker decided I was still not in a fit state to look after them. I knew in my heart of hearts it was the right decision. I was still fragile, dependent on welfare and afraid that the same downward spiral would overcome me again if I was put under undue stress. I was assured that the boys and Clare were doing fine – and was delighted to hear that Clare was going to school and had made new friends.

But I was desolate on my own in the flat. I knew very few people in Mullingar and my self-confidence was at zero. Once more I decided to leave Ireland. My children were settled, and coping, it seemed, without me. To all intents and purposes I was never going to get them back. I had a psychiatric record, I'd reduced the daughter I loved to living on the streets, and had failed to be a stable influence in the lives of my boys. I'd come from a disruptive and dysfunctional family and had continued the pattern. The only difference was that I adored my children and wanted what was best for them.

Time dragged on and nothing changed. My mother was totally fed up with my depression and anxious for me to move on with my life. I thought of going to London and finding work there. When I told her of my plan to leave, she contacted a friend, and through a friend of that friend, I was offered a place to stay until I found somewhere to settle. My mother encouraged me to go and make a fresh start in a new environment. But as I packed to leave I realised I was doing exactly what she had done with us all of our lives. I was running away any time I felt under pressure, constantly running away from my problems – and I couldn't seem to stop myself.

Fifteen

New Beginnings

The man who offered me accommodation was called
Abdullah. He was a Muslim and was originally from
Lebanon. He had lived for many years in London and
when we'd spoken on the phone, he'd assured me that
his apartment was spacious. There would be plenty of
room for me.

We met, as arranged, at Heathrow airport. Our sign
of recognition was a bunch of white roses, though
romance was the last thing on my mind. His English
was perfect and he put me at my ease as he drove to his
apartment just off the Harrow Road. He was a much-
travelled man with an extended family living in
Lebanon and in many parts of continental Europe. His

apartment was much smaller than I'd imagined, but it was clean and offered me a roof over my head. He shared it with his younger brother, a quiet, courteous young man with whom I got on well.

When I could afford it, I travelled to Ireland to see my children, but my life situation remained difficult and my depression showed no signs of lifting. On the return flight from one such visit home I found it hard to stay in my seat before the plane took off. I'd stand up to ask the cabin crew to let me off the plane, then sink down again, knowing I had nowhere else to go.

As my relationship with Abdullah progressed, we became lovers and I soon discovered I was pregnant. On the night I broke the news to him, we walked for miles across London, discussing what we should do. We finally reached a decision. We would marry. Abdullah had a dominant personality, but he was also charming and persuasive. I imagined he was offering me a chance at stability. I couldn't forget the terror of being homeless and living on the streets, and still hoped that, with time, I could bring my children together again. As my mother had encouraged me to do, I was making a fresh start. I really believed this marriage could work if I gave it my best shot.

I've often wondered since then if that pregnancy, although unplanned, was, on some level, a form of wish fulfilment to make up for the children I'd left behind. But it was not to be. Despite having a healthy, normal pregnancy, I lost the baby, a boy, at seven months. Giving birth to a child who is lifeless and yet looks absolutely perfect is heartbreaking. The birth is just the same, but for the grief that awaits you. I cried as I held my beautiful little boy in my arms. The hospital staff dressed him in baby clothes and they took pictures of him, and of his father and I holding him, so that we would always have something to remember him by, with love. He was perfectly developed, but small. It was a terrible day. Abdullah was visibly upset and cried bitterly.

We went home afterwards in a taxi. It was obvious to the taxi driver that I was dreadfully upset. He recognised me, and it turned out that he had been a friend of my father. They'd worked together in Coolure House. Meeting the taxi driver added to my homesickness and sense of bereavement. I had to do something to lift myself from the inevitable depression that followed my loss.

In April 2003, on the advice of a friend, I visited a psychiatrist, Dr Roy Shuttleworth, to be assessed for a disability living allowance. I explained my medical history and listed the medication I'd been on over the years. He was shocked but understanding, and asked if I wanted to go to him for therapy. I hadn't a penny to my name but he said it didn't matter. He believed he could help me and he wanted to try.

During our sessions he explained that it was perfectly normal to feel such guilt and helplessness over my father's death. I'd lived with the lie for so long because I'd believed I had no other option. When I told him about my second overdose – after I'd decided to put Clare into care – he said that I had been on an emotional rollercoaster since the murder and such breakdowns had been inevitable. They had occurred when I was at the height of my pain. He was a tremendous support and helped me to understand myself a little better.

He wrote the following report in 2003 and I've held on to it as a kind of validation of why I was the way I was. Now, when I read it, I can hardly believe I was at such a low ebb.

Clinical State: Ms McGrath is suffering from two serious psychiatric conditions, mainly Clinical Depression and Post Traumatic Stress Disorder.

For Clinical Depression she needs to have five out of a possible nine symptoms; she has all nine.

i) Depressed mood most of the time. She said that on a 10 point scale with 1 being as low as you could go and ten being as happy as you could be, that her mood during the session was at the 1 out of 10 level. She said her normal range is between 1 and 3.

ii) She has a markedly diminished interest and pleasure in most activities most of the day. She said there was little that actually gives her any interest or pleasure.

iii) Her appetite is very variable. On occasions

she will overeat and put weight on and then has very little appetite and will become underweight.

iv) Insomnia: she has great difficulty in getting off to sleep and will wake early. She has frequent nightmares.

v) She is very psychomotor-retarded, generally feeling very low. Generally feels fatigued and loss of energy

vi) She feels worthless and has inappropriate guilt, for example not being able to save her father from being killed.

vii) She has difficulty in thinking and is generally indecisive..

viii) She frequently feels that she would be better off dead with very strong urges every few weeks.

ix) Has had several overdose attempts over the years with the last in 2001.

In relation to Post Traumatic Stress Disorder he wrote:

(1) She experienced an event which involved actual or threatened death or serious injury to herself and others.

(2) Her response involved intense fear, helplessness and horror. At one stage she thought that both she and her brothers could be murdered.

Criteria:
She experienced all five aspects of these criteria.

(1) Recurrent and intrusive distressing recollections of the event: These happen in a variable way between three and four times a week to once a month. In particular she remembers her father's cut-off head lying on the ground and being forced the next day to go and wash away the gore left behind at the killing spot. She said she sometimes hears his death gargle and her mother laughing.

(2) Recurring distressing dreams of the event. These happen between two and seven times a week. They either represent a replay of actual events or a frightening dream where two figures come running after her.

(3) Acting or feeling as if the traumatic events were recurring. She said on occasion when she is walking in open spaces the whole event will come back to her as if it is happening again and she will have to run to escape from it.

(4) Intense psychological distress and exposure to internal and external cues that symbolise or resemble an aspect of the traumatic event. She said this is sometimes triggered off by a television or radio programme involving violence or murder. She said this is normally three or four times a month or if her mood is low it will be at least twice a week.

(5) Physiological reactivity on exposure to internal or external cues that symbolise or resemble an aspect of the traumatic event.

She said that when she is in contact with these thoughts she will shake, cry, feels very nervous, has a beating heart, sweats and if it occurs whilst she is in bed she will often lose control of her bladder and then continue to lie in the wet because she is too scared to get up.

That report distresses me to this day. It also makes me angry. I should never have been that person. But I was trapped by the past and it was destroying my life.

Abdullah and I decided we would still get married, and to do this I needed to divorce Colin Pinder. My brief marriage to him seemed like a long-ago dream and I only ever thought of him now as one of my father's killers. He didn't contest the action and within weeks he had signed the papers.

I married Abdullah in the autumn of 2003. I bought a beautiful second-hand wedding dress in a charity shop. It was entirely different from the outfit I'd worn the first time – and I shut my mind to the circumstances surrounding that occasion. Some days before we were due to be at the registry office, Abdullah told me we had to attend a mosque. I thought this was because he was marrying a Catholic and needed the blessing of the imam to do so. On our way to a mosque near Edgware Road, he stopped at a market stall and bought a veil to cover my hair. I wasn't used to wearing a *hijab* and I had to keep pushing my hair out of sight.

A number of men and the imam were waiting for us

in the mosque. I was taken into a room where they prayed in Arabic. I couldn't follow what they were saying but I heard the imam mention something about 'change'. He was asking me to convert to Islam and to honour Ramadan. I told him I didn't want to change my religion. I'd been baptised a Catholic and wanted to remain one. My refusal upset him. I went with Abdullah into another room where he explained the procedure and assured me everything would be okay.

I still believed we were receiving a blessing and we returned to the room where more prayers were recited in Arabic. After we left the mosque, Abdullah told us we'd just been married in a Muslim ceremony. That was a bolt from the blue – I'd had no idea I was getting married – but I knew that Abdullah's religious beliefs were important to him and I still believed we could be happy together. A few days later, on 20 August 2003, which was the date of my father's birthday, I wore my wedding dress to the old Marylebone town hall where we were married for the second time. The wedding party was small. My friend and her husband attended, also Abdullah's brother and cousin. Abdullah's friend videoed the ceremony and we ended the day in a Lebanese restaurant.

Our cultural differences were hard to overcome but I did my best to cope with them. I became used to buying food in halal shops and cooking to Abdullah's specifications. I watched Muslim television channels and made sure not to walk around the house in my pyjamas or anything too casual if his brother was around.

I became pregnant again shortly after our wedding and gave birth to a beautiful little girl in July 2004. We called her Natalia. She was stunning, with olive skin, black hair and dark eyes. Shortly after her birth I was pregnant again and, in 2005, had another beautiful daughter, whom we called Jade. After her birth, the housework started to catch up with me – with two tiny children, it was hard to keep the house to Abdullah's high standards. This annoyed him and I became increasingly stressed as time went by.

On two occasions we visited his family in Lebanon. They lived in a beautiful village called Bajaria and the large, extended family lived together in an apartment block. The first time, before we left England, Abdullah told me how the women dressed and behaved in his country. I was nervous, aware that I did not conform to the traditions of his society. But I wanted to meet his family and was excited about the trip. When we arrived in Bajaria, the men in his family expected me to wear a long robe. Out of respect, I agreed to cover my head with the customary *hijab* but refused to cover myself from head to toe. It was obvious that the men ruled the roost.

Abdullah's sister was beautiful. She had been very young when their mother had died but she had taken over as the family's mother figure and, therefore, had never married. With the help of an Arabic–English dictionary, she did her best to talk to me. She'd take off her veil when she came into my bedroom, but as soon as she heard someone coming, she would rush to put it back on. Other members of Abdullah's extended family lived in Europe and we visited them all. Wherever we went – Sweden, Germany, Switzerland – we lived within a strict Islamic code, and my life was not so very different at home.

In May 2008, five years after my marriage to Abdullah, I received an astonishing phone call from a detective in Ireland. He introduced himself as Detective Garda Dave O'Brien, a member of the Garda Serious Crime Review Team, also known as the cold-case team, led by Superintendent Christy Mangan. It had been formed in 2007 to look into murder cases that had remained unresolved since 1980. Forensic testing had developed considerably over the intervening years and positive results were being achieved. They intended investigating my father's death. 'We want to bury your daddy,' the detective said. I could hardly believe my ears.

I told him that my father had been buried in Whitehall Cemetery since 1998. He seemed surprised by this information but said an exhumation of my father's remains would be necessary for DNA testing and other procedures. I hated the thought of my father's grave being disturbed, but this was another opportunity for him to receive his long-awaited justice.

I would later discover that Detective Garda John Maunsell, now retired, had requested that my father's case be reopened and considered for further investigation. The fact that Brian McGrath never knew his mother and father, never knew if he had sisters or brothers, bloodline siblings who would demand to know where he was after he 'deserted' my mother, made this a particularly poignant case, and the team of investigators was anxious to solve it.

After the phone call ended I collapsed into a chair, my head in a spin. I'd been told that some of the cold-case team hoped to interview me in London and they would be in touch soon again. It was fourteen years since I'd first confided my story to Pauline, eleven years since my mother had waved the letter in my face and announced that there would be no prosecution. I didn't know whether to be relieved or worried. A chain of events over which I had had no control had been set in motion. Because of the previous police investigation, I knew exactly what would be involved – and it was scary. Coole would be in the news again. The media would be on the scent. The field would be dug up once more. And my mother ... Just thinking about her reaction caused me to break into a cold sweat. I'd no idea if she knew the case had been reopened and, if she had been told, whether she thought I was responsible. The more I thought about it, the more worried I became. But in the meantime I had two children and a home to look after. I collected my thoughts. I knew it was important not to get my hopes up. There was a long road ahead and I wasn't confident that the result would be any different from the last time.

I suddenly had an overwhelming urge to be in Coole. I needed to be where all my troubles had begun. I left the children in their father's care and bought a ticket home.

When I arrived, the house in Coole was like a tinderbox. My mother was reeling from the news that the case had been reopened. She blamed me for stirring it up and refused to believe that I was as shocked as she was. I discovered that the cold-case team had contacted my three brothers around the same time and requested that they provide DNA samples. She'd been furious to hear this, and furious, I'm sure, that the past had caught up with her. I was the last person she wanted to see. We had a blazing row and she accused me of setting out to destroy her life.

I fled the house in the small hours, without even collecting my possessions, and contacted my brother Andrew, who lived in Galway at the time. He drove immediately to Coole. I waited for him in the church and we headed back to Galway together. As we neared Roscommon, his phone rang. Garda Dave O'Brien told him that the cold-case team had begun their work. Officers were in the cemetery ready to exhume my father's remains, which would be brought to the Dublin City morgue for examination. They hoped the

DNA tests would definitively establish my father's identity and give them the answers they needed.

When Garda O'Brien realised I was in the car beside Andrew, he asked to speak to me. We arranged that I would be interviewed at Andrew's house later in the morning. Events were moving fast and I hadn't had time to absorb the full significance of the investigation. I recalled the horror of the last occasion, the trauma and grief we had endured, and the long-drawn-out wait for a decision to be made on whether or not someone would be charged with our father's murder. I was older now but the emotions were the same.

Soon after we arrived at Andrew's house I was interviewed by two detectives. They showed me the pictures I'd drawn in 1993, when I was first interviewed by the British police at the women's refuge in Liverpool. I looked at the pen drawings of the slash hooks and the balustrades and was amazed they had been kept on record for so long. I was interviewed for hours, questioned repeatedly over the tiniest details. Twenty-one years had passed since the night of my father's murder but my memory of those horrifying scenes was still vivid. I felt sick and had to visit the bathroom several times to throw up.

I was asked to return to Coole the following day to go over the scene of the crime. From my last experience, I had some idea of what to expect from the media – but nothing could have prepared me for the scene that greeted us. Cars and vans were parked all along the main road off our side road. They were also parked in a field opposite our piece of land, which we called the Horse Field, though there were no horses that day. I saw a television van with monitors showing various sites on our field where Gardaí were working. Our arrival created even more mayhem. Journalists and photographers jostled for our attention as we approached the house.

My mother had left the house. Some years previously she had moved to Clougherboy in Navan so I assumed that was where she intended staying until the dig was finished and the media had moved on. The guards accompanied me to the back of the house where shiny new slash hooks of all makes and sizes had been lined up in rows. A woman wearing white forensics coveralls and carrying a camera approached and asked me to point to the slash hook Colin Pinder had used to attack my father. When I pointed to an identical one, it was photographed and tagged.

The entire contents of the kitchen had been moved outside. When I entered the empty room, the only thing still in place was the range. I was asked by the guards if this was the range my father had fallen against and hit his head on during the night he died. I didn't understand the question. My father had never entered the house on the night he was killed, as I'd made perfectly clear in the many interviews I'd given. But the questions about the range continued. This was my first inkling that Colin Pinder had told the police a different story from mine when he was interviewed in 1993.

Showing them around the exterior of the house brought its own difficulties. Changes had been made to it over the years. The bedroom window my mother had climbed through was now fronted by an extension, and the driveway had been lengthened. More photographs were taken at various locations where my father had fallen. Then I was brought to the field towards the scene of the dig. Unlike the last time when the entire field was dug up, the guards were digging only in sections. They asked me to walk around with them and point out exactly where the grave had been dug and the fire lit. The land had been in better condition in 1993 and it was difficult now to point to precise sites. More photographs were taken of me at each location and numbered tags were stuck into the ground to identify the crime scenes.

As I walked around the field, reliving the horror of that distant time, I began to feel sick and dizzy and collapsed. The guards sat me up and allowed me time to recover. They had some water and handed me a bottle to drink. I felt a little better, but still nauseous when I stood up. They had planned to bring me to the lane outside the house where my father had tried to hide, but it was swarming with photographers and journalists. Instead, I stayed in the house until the media had gone. Then Andrew and I were free to leave. My father's case was on television, radio and in the papers. It's difficult to describe the feeling of being under siege – but that day was only a taster of what was to come.

I spent a few days in Galway, well beyond the reach of the media. I had an old car that Andrew kept for me when I was in London. I drove it back to Coole when I believed the coast was clear.

My mother had returned to the house. Liam, now a young man of nineteen, had been living with her and her partner in Coole before news had broken of the investigation, and I was anxious about how he was coping with this upheaval in his life. I hoped to see him, and also wanted to make clear to Vera that I'd had no hand in reopening the case. When I arrived at the house, the gates were locked. She'd erected them before the investigation began, and now when anyone arrived, they had to beep their horn before she'd open them. She refused to let me in. I rang Liam on his mobile and asked him to come outside. He arrived to the gates and told me that Vera didn't want to see me. We talked for a while, and he agreed to collect my few possessions for me.

From Coole I drove to Longford, where I rented a room for a few days to try to get my head together. I felt exhausted, still suffering bouts of nausea and – apart from the stress of the investigation – I was very worried about my marriage. I knew it was over. It was not just the religious and cultural differences that had made things difficult over the five years we had been together. He was a controlling, dominating man who was violent on occasion, and abusive to me both physically and mentally. I had been living in fear. I had joined a support group called Woman's Trust, where I had learned some coping skills. Although I was still scared of my husband, I'd learned how to have some control over that fear.

Our relationship had by now reached the stage where I had to decide whether to stay and endure the life he imposed on me or to seek a divorce. But I dreaded the custodial battle over our two daughters that would likely follow. Now I had the situation at Coole to consider, too, and the possibility of another long-drawn-out investigation.

But when the bouts of sickness continued and I realised I was pregnant again, I knew it was time to return to my husband for a serious discussion about our future. Before I left Ireland, I tried once more to contact my mother. To my surprise, she agreed to see me and allowed me to stay overnight. She had calmed down and we were able to discuss the investigation without another row. I also told her my news.

The following day I flew back to London.

Sixteen

Breaking Point

Abdullah knew the circumstances of my father's death – we'd talked about it in the early stages of our relationship. But there was no avoiding the happenings in Coole. It had been hard to cope with the media attention, the intense Garda questioning, my brothers' shock and distress, and my mother's suspicions that I was at the heart of it all. Added to this, I was forty and pregnant again. I had a lot on my mind as I greeted my daughters and husband.

The girls were delighted to see me. They wanted to know about Coole and when they could go there with me for a holiday. Natalia had been there once but only as a baby so she had no memory of meeting her grandmother. When they were settled for the night, I told Abdullah about the latest developments. The flat, quiet except for our voices, seemed a million miles from the bedlam I'd left behind. I also told him I was pregnant. He was pleased and believed we should try again to make our marriage work. I agreed, but wondered if another baby would be enough to cement our shaky relationship. I hoped so. The shock of the investigation had made me realise how vulnerable I was. I needed someone supportive behind me over the next few years if my mother and Colin Pinder were sent for trial. Also, my children and the new life growing inside me needed a father. I knew to my cost the hardship involved in trying to bring up children without one.

With another baby on the way, we needed more space. Abdullah promised to rent a bigger house or apartment. Over the next few weeks, I viewed a number of properties. But the difficulties that had dogged our marriage in the past continued.

After a particularly stressful period, I realised I could no longer stay with him. We parted and I left the flat, taking our two daughters with me. We were provided with council accommodation and I began divorce proceedings.

Around this time, I became particularly anxious about Liam back home in Coole. His father, Colin Pinder, would be a key figure in the ongoing investigation and I was worried about how my eldest son would cope with the issues that arose from this difficult situation. I told Abdullah that I was taking the children with me to Ireland, and he raised no objections. It was hard to leave my council flat – in doing so I was making myself intentionally homeless, as it was termed – but I needed to be at home with Liam.

For obvious reasons, I didn't want to live in the family home. I bought a mobile home and my mother allowed me to take it on to the land. I organised my own electricity with a lead coming from a socket in the kitchen, and arranged separate bill payments. I also had my own water supply. Over the following weeks, I set about making our new home as comfortable as possible. I enrolled Natalia in the local school I'd once attended and Jade joined a Montessori.

Andrew had moved from Galway back to Coole and was staying temporarily in a caravan beside mine. Liam moved in with him and we tried to live as normally as possible in an abnormal environment. But the uncertainty was nerve-racking. My mother's anxiety was obvious and she often took to her bed for long periods. She found it particularly difficult to deal with the mounting publicity and wore a wig and dark glasses when she went out in public. I lived a cat-and-mouse existence, staying out of sight in the mobile home when I saw her outside and trying to keep the children from making noise and annoying her. Despite all this, though, we had moments of togetherness and she would even confide her worries to me – about the possibility of prison and how she would cope with it. When the weather was particularly cold, she allowed us to use the spare bedroom. She'd developed an eye problem and I'd apply her drops in the evening. Once Andrew and I clubbed together and sent her for a beauty treatment, which cheered her up for a while. For the most part, though, the atmosphere was like a pressure cooker, and flare-ups were inevitable.

My mother still travelled between Navan and Coole, staying in her house in Navan with her partner for weeks. Her absences allowed us to catch our breath and relax, as far as that was possible.

In November 2008, I was seven months pregnant, and my mother was back living in Coole. One morning, having spent the night in the spare bedroom with the two girls, I went into the kitchen and knew immediately that she was on edge. This would be one of the dark days. I decided to take the kids and head for my mobile home before a row began. I first went to the bathroom, and when I emerged I saw a guard in uniform standing in the kitchen. I should have been used to their presence in our house but there was something different this time. Other guards entered the small, low-ceilinged room and suddenly it seemed crowded with men in uniform.

My mother was told she would be brought to Mullingar Garda Station for questioning. I hadn't wanted to be present when she was arrested. It didn't matter how often I told myself that she was responsible for her crime: on some level I still felt enormous guilt for breaking that vow of silence. She was accompanied by a female Garda when she went into her bedroom to dress. She asked me to find her eyedrops. It was such a simple thing to remember at such a terrible time. I hadn't expected to feel sorry for her – too much bad history behind us – but I did. I also felt guilty for having gone to the police in the first place. At the end of the day, she would always be my mother, the only one I had. I'd lost my father and now it was becoming a real possibility that I would lose her too.

Her partner had left earlier on an errand. She must have rung him because he returned shortly and set about contacting her solicitor. I recognised one of the guards from the investigation. He greeted me by my first name and asked how life was treating me. His manner was friendly but his timing couldn't have been worse: my mother, dressed and made-up, had just walked into the kitchen. I froze, convinced it would add to her suspicions that I was responsible for resurrecting the case. 'Can't you see how we are?' I snapped, but it didn't matter. My mother would always blame me for destroying her life.

Members of the cold-case team were waiting outside. Official procedure did not allow them to issue the arrest warrant. This had to be issued by the local superintendent.

My mother was taken to Mullingar and questioned.

189

Later she was released without charge. She was extremely annoyed and upset when she returned to Coole. The media had been waiting outside the Garda station to photograph her when she came out. We did our best to calm her down but she only spoke to me when it was absolutely necessary. One of the lads prepared a big fry-up and we sat down together to eat it. The situation was unreal, all of us sharing food around a table, all of us trapped in our own emotions and thoughts. I'd questioned her so many times about the night she murdered my father. I'd demanded reasons, answers, an explanation that would make sense of the madness that had possessed her and Colin. Those discussions always ended in a row. She would lash out verbally at me for daring to bring up the subject or she'd retreat into silence and simply refuse to speak about it.

My fourth daughter, Amy, was born in January 2009. She was overdue and I took a taxi to the hospital where I was induced. The baby had breathing problems so I had to stay in hospital for three days while family friends minded the two older girls. My mother came to visit me and I appreciated the effort it must have cost her. Although she had no idea how the case was progressing, she knew that it was only a matter of time before she heard something, and no doubt the wait was an anxious one.

On Thursday, 5 February 2009, we heard that Colin Pinder had arrived in Ireland to be questioned. He was taken to Mullingar Garda Station and charged with the murder of Brian McGrath at a special sitting of Athlone District Court the following day. He was then remanded in custody. The court ordered that the necessary epilepsy drugs were to be supplied to him in prison, and he was to have a psychiatric and medical assessment. The events were extensively covered by the media. I hadn't seen Colin since he'd left me all those years ago. He was now forty-six years old and I could hardly bring myself to look at the television screen. He was in handcuffs and seemed petrified. His eyes were red. To my surprise, I felt a surge of sympathy for him. I thought back to the early days of our relationship, the happy times we'd shared together before my mother had discovered where I was staying. What had possessed him that night to take the life of a man he hardly knew? I'd never understood it and, as with my mother, he'd never been able to give me a satisfactory explanation.

But my immediate concern was for Liam, who had no memory of his father and was in tears as he watched the television. This was another extremely difficult time for everyone concerned and we could only wait anxiously to see what happened next.

As the weeks passed, my mother's mood grew darker and more threatening. I was the lightning rod for her anger. On one occasion she attacked my mobile home with a sledgehammer, then began throwing logs at it. I heard the banging and looked out, unable to believe my eyes. Another time, she cut off my electricity and restricted the flow of water. The fact that I had young daughters and a small baby didn't stop her – and there was no talking to her when she was in one of those moods. I spent most of my time with the girls in the mobile home, dreading the next eruption. I used candles at night, and we drank bottled water.

Liam was a great help with the new baby. I was glad to share this time with him. It was a relief when Vera stayed in Navan with her partner and we could relax for a short while.

On one such night I moved into the house with the kids. The weather was bitterly cold and I was worried about them. We slept in the spare bedroom but my mother and her partner arrived back unexpectedly. When she realised I was in the house she was furious, though she didn't try to evict us. Later, after her partner was in bed, I heard her calling me. When I ran into the kitchen the curtains were on fire. She had deliberately set them alight. Her eyes were glazed and unfocused as I filled a basin and flung water over the flames. Eventually the fire went out. My mother was beside herself with rage, and I feared for her sanity. When she finally went to bed I lay awake for the rest of the night, listening for the slightest sound from her room.

It seemed that things could hardly get worse – but they did. She lost her temper one night when I called into the house. She screamed at me, flinging anything to hand in my direction. Cups and plates were smashed and I was worried for the safety of the girls. I texted a neighbour for help. I'd asked him earlier if I could borrow a spare gas cylinder from him, and now he arrived with it. He saw at a glance that things were far from good, but the sight of him forced my mother to calm down.

After she'd gone to bed, I sat up with Andrew until three in the morning trying to decide what to do. I wanted to leave, but with three small children, I'd nowhere to stay in London. I'd quit my council flat voluntarily so had no hope of being rehoused. My divorce from Abdullah had come through so returning to him was out of the question. Later I tried to sleep but I was too upset to manage more than a fitful doze.

Early in the morning I heard voices outside. When I looked out the window I saw that the Gardaí had arrived again. They followed the same procedure as before. The cold-case team waited outside and Detective Inspector Martin Cadden told my mother that she was being arrested in connection with the murder of her husband. Anything she said would be written down and used in evidence against her.

I was petrified, convinced that if she was released again, there'd be a repeat performance of the previous night. I confided my fears to one of the guards. He reassured me that although she would be allowed out on bail she would be warned that if she went near me, or caused any further trouble, her bail would be revoked. He believed she wouldn't do anything to risk that. I was worried in case the girls saw their grandmother being taken away but everything was done quickly and within a few minutes she left under police escort.

Later she was brought to Longford District Court. There Detective Inspector Cadden said he had arrested her at her home at 8.10 a.m. and brought her to Mullingar Garda Station where she was formally charged. As she had feared, she was remanded in custody and taken to Mountjoy Jail where she spent the following seven days. On her release she came to the house to collect some possessions before returning to attend Longford District Court.

I stayed out of sight in the mobile home with the girls, nervous in case another row broke out. She was told that her bail would be revoked if she did anything to upset or hurt me. She gathered what she needed and left for the court. I watched from the window as she got back into the car with her partner and they drove off. I was hugely relieved to see her go.

At Longford District Court she was granted bail with no conditions set. That was the last time she visited Coole. Prior to the trial, she stayed in Fordstown in Navan with her partner.

I was informed by the guards that I would be a witness for the prosecution. When we were waiting for the trial to begin, a guard involved in the investigation advised me to break my ties with my mother. Taking the stand in court and giving evidence against her would be traumatic, he warned. I didn't need to hear that to know it was true. Every fibre of my being warned me that this would be horrible. As the chief prosecution witness, I was not offered any protection from prosecution. Neither did I receive advice or counselling on how I could cope with giving evidence against my mother and my ex-husband. The trial was now set to begin on Monday, 14 June 2010.

Abdullah had been in touch with me on a number of occasions. He missed his daughters and had not yet seen Amy. Like me, he was desperately worried about the forthcoming trial and how it would impact on the children. They had already been exposed to the presence of uniformed guards arriving at the house and my mother's uncontrollable rages. Also, I knew how invasive the media would be. This was the first cold-case trial to be brought to court and it would attract widespread coverage. I hated the thought of my children having to deal with journalists or photographers waiting outside the house. Despite our best efforts to protect them from the media coverage, I was afraid they would see pictures of their mother and grandmother entering or leaving the court. I'd been told that I had to attend court every day of the trial so I wouldn't be at home to give them the protection they needed. I was afraid Natalia might pick up on remarks made by other children in school, or overhear comments from adults.

Abdullah pleaded with me to come to London and discuss what could be done. I agreed, and he met the girls and me at the airport. We returned to the flat. He apologised for having caused me so much distress in the past. Once again, he was prepared to make a fresh start and offered to mind the two older girls until the trial was over. Any notion of beginning again with him had long since left me, but I knew that it was better for Natalia and Jade to be away from Coole for the duration of the trial and so, heartbroken, I decided to leave them in their father's care. I would keep the baby with me in Coole and return to London as soon as the trial ended. I'd been told it would last about three weeks.

It was lashing rain when I left the flat and travelled to the airport with Amy. I thought about my boys, Liam and Bernard, both in contact with me again – but young adults now, determined to go their own way in life. I wondered what troubled memories they carried from their childhood and if they blamed me for the lack of contact with their fathers. I thought of Clare, a sweet, good-natured child, still in foster care: would she ever understand the hard road I'd travelled with her and the heartbreaking decisions I'd made in her best interests? I thought of the two little daughters I'd left with their father, a man I no longer loved but was now dependent on. As I sat in the airport I had a terrible premonition that they, too, might slip through my hands. I fought off this feeling of dread and boarded the plane to Ireland.

Seventeen

The Trial

I'd seen it so often on television – the victims and the accused facing the cameras when they arrived or left the Central Criminal Court in Dublin. As I waited for the trial date to arrive, a knot would tighten in my stomach as I watched such scenes, knowing that soon I would have to take that walk. I kept myself busy in the lead-up. I put in place child-minding arrangements for Amy and brought her for long walks around Coole. I knew the local community was horrified – understandably – by the events that had happened so long ago and that were now being dragged into the open. I felt very alone and humiliated. Our neighbours had always been kind to me but they must have wondered about the night of my father's murder, and whether I'd played a part. But Coole was only a small section of the much larger community I'd face in court. I needed to clear my head and focus on the trial. But the more I thought about what lay ahead, the more frightened I became.

The trial began on Monday, 14 June 2010, in the Central Criminal Court, Dublin. I left Amy with friends and drove into Mullingar. From there I took the train to Connolly station in Dublin, then the Luas to Smithfield. As I was standing at traffic lights, about to cross the road to the courthouse, I got my first glimpse of Colin Pinder in the flesh, heading to it from the opposite direction with another man. I hadn't seen my ex-husband in person in over twenty years, and though he had changed a lot – his head was shaven and he looked much older than I remembered - his tall figure was instantly recognisable. He looked smart and polished in a suit and tie. It seemed incredible that we had once shared a bed, produced a child, laughed and been happy together, if only for a brief time. I didn't know if he'd seen me and I didn't wait to find out. I quickly crossed the road.

The Central Criminal Court is a magnificent new building, only open since late 2009. It looks to me like a luxury hotel. There's so much glass in the design that my first impression on entering was of stepping into an enormous goldfish bowl. As I climbed the marble stairs to the first floor, I glanced out through the glass wall and saw my mother sitting in an enclosed garden-like area for smokers. I hadn't seen her for about eight months and had been dreading the moment when we'd meet again. Before I could look away she glanced up and saw me. Our eyes locked for an instant before she turned away. Within a few minutes I'd seen the two people I'd most dreaded meeting. I took deep breaths and told myself that the first hurdle was over.

I did my best to keep calm, but sitting in the court café was no easier. When I walked towards a table with my coffee, I saw Colin and his companion. Moving to the other side of the café, I faced my mother and her partner. The only other familiar face belonged to Detective Inspector Cadden, who'd arrested my mother on a charge of murder all those months ago in Coole. We exchanged a few words but I was conscious that she would see me talking to him and it would confirm her suspicions that I in cahoots with the authorities.

At one stage during a break in the day's proceedings I saw her sitting alone in the café. She looked lost and vulnerable, especially as a female journalist was seated in her direct line of vision, staring fixedly at her, as if she wanted to record every facial expression, every movement she made. I was about to order a coffee for myself but, on a sudden impulse, I veered towards my mother's table. I'd been advised against it by the Gardaí but I couldn't help myself. I asked if she'd like a caffè latte, her favourite coffee. She turned her head away – I can still see the swish of her hair – and never answered me. I walked away from her, knowing that our relationship, with all its hurt and bitterness, was finished for ever.

I was introduced to Noreen, a member of the court services, who was kind and supportive throughout the trial. She helped me to get my bearings, showed me the entrance I could use that would help me to avoid meeting Colin Pinder or my mother, the route that would take me to the witness stand – again avoiding face-to-face contact.

My mother and Colin Pinder pleaded not guilty to the murder of my father. When they appeared again the following Friday, 18 June, Colin had changed his plea to guilty of manslaughter. The state refused to accept his manslaughter plea. My father's murder was the first cold case to be prosecuted and Justice John Edwards told the jury to steer away from any printed or broadcast reports on the case. He warned them that they were not allowed to look up any old news reports, information on Google or reports on what had happened in the run-up to the trial. The media had a keen interest in the result. So also had the public, who were fascinated by the details and crowded into the courtroom every day.

Taking the stand to be examined by the prosecution counsel on the third day of the trial was even more intimidating than I'd expected. Not that I'd expected an easy time – I'd been well warned in advance. My legs were trembling so much that I wasn't sure they'd carry me to the stand. Prosecution counsel Denis Vaughan Buckley brought me through the events that had haunted me since I was eighteen years old. My mother cried throughout my evidence. I felt as if I was being torn in two. I wanted the truth to come out but my father was dead. It didn't matter to him one way or the other. My mother was alive and I was destroying her life. I wanted to run from the court with my hands over my ears and hide somewhere until everything bad in my life disappeared.

I held my nerve and described the night in question and the series of events leading to my father's death. I described the fire, how long it had burned, the smell that I've never been able to forget, the images I still cannot banish. Mr Buckley allowed me the time to explain my relationship with Colin Pinder and how difficult my life had been since that night.

The following days were to prove harder than my worst imaginings. Patrick Gageby SC, who was defending my mother, put it to me that I was portraying myself as an innocent witness. 'By your failure to act, you might be more involved in your father's death,' he said. 'I suggest you placed your mother as a prime conspirator and painted yourself as the good guy when perhaps you aren't. I suggest you tend to be rather manipulative and you've implicated your mother to disguise your own guilt. I suggest you were not the vulnerable witness then or now and that it's not your mother who's dominant, but you,' he said.

He brought me through my private life, my moves between Ireland and England, my relationships with the fathers of my children. He referred to the fact that I'd returned to Coole many times since 1987 and suggested that this was strange behaviour for someone who was haunted by the events that had taken place there. I knew how my messed-up life must seem to those looking at it from the outside. There were times I wished I could have given a proper account of myself, made clear that I wasn't a bad person, a liar, a conspirator. But I had to answer the questions put to me by the defence without elaboration. I wasn't there to explain my crazy life, or the psychological reasons, which I barely understood myself, why I would return to the home of the woman who was at the root of all my problems – yet the only person in the world who truly understood them.

When Mr Gageby suggested I'd spun a story that put me in a good light and my mother in a bad one, I became emotional on the stand and began to cry. 'I suggest you're a person who does try to suit yourself and never let anything get in the way of what you want,' he said. He also suggested that I had a rose-tinted memory of my father and had actually made complaints against him when I was a teenager. I denied this and denied also that my father frequently threatened to kill my mother and put her in the septic tank.

It seemed as if he'd no sooner sat down than Conor

Devally SC, defending Colin Pinder, was on his feet to question me about my father being committed to a psychiatric hospital for a week in 1985. I recalled the doctor being in the house before my father was taken to St Loman's in Mullingar but could not remember him examining bruises on me. He suggested that not being able to remember this and other details about the incident was because I'd been party to having him committed.

I denied this but I could feel the atmosphere in the court bearing down on me. At one stage in the cross-examination I was so distressed the judge granted a recess until I had had a drink of water and composed myself. Noreen encouraged me to be strong and helped me feel that I could withstand the cross-examination. 'Roll with the punches,' she advised.

I spent five days in the witness box. During that time the version of events that Colin Pinder had told the guards was revealed to the jury by Mr Devally. He suggested that a row had erupted when my father came home on the night of his death to find myself and Colin in the house with my mother. By this version of events, my father called Colin racist names and ordered him out of the house. As a result of this abuse, Colin lost his temper and hit him hard. My father struck his head off the range as he fell. Colin thought he'd killed him. He had claimed that it was decided between the three of us not to call the guards and that we moved him outside, but when my mother found out he was still alive, she goaded Colin into hitting him again. He had claimed that I came out and took turns with my mother to hit my father.

I listened in disbelief as his statement was outlined before myself and the jury. Until then I hadn't been fully aware of the version of events he'd told the police during his investigation in 1993. I denied the accusations he'd made, and when Mr Devally asked if I remembered telling Colin that he'd never see our baby if he called the police on the night of the murder, I insisted that I wasn't pregnant at the time. I also denied using my pregnancy to persuade Colin to move to Ireland and marry me.

Outside our family circle, my father was last seen alive on 10 March 1987 when he stopped to talk to a guard near his home. After that he was never seen again in the community. I married Colin on 18 April – and that is another definite date. Although I cannot be sure of the exact date of my father's murder, he was dead and buried weeks before we married on 18 April. Our son was born on 24 December 1987. At the time of my father's death, it is very unlikely that I was pregnant, but even if I was, I certainly could not possibly have known about it.

Mr Devally put it to me that the story of the killing I'd told the jury was something that I and maybe my mother had cooked up in the years that followed. I denied this and was challenged on why I'd helped her to get a barring order on my father after he was dead.

I answered these questions as best I could but, again, there was no opportunity to elaborate on the dominant role she had always played in my life. I felt punch drunk as the questions kept coming, and I just rolled with them as best I could.

One evening, when I arrived home after another day of cross-examination, I was so exhausted from the constant questioning that I rang Detective Maunsell and told him I didn't think I could cope with the pressure any more. He was closely watching each stage of the trial and he reassured me that I was bearing up well. He advised me to stay strong and positive. His words were reassuring. He'd believed me all those years ago and his belief in my story was still strong. But the night terrors still came with the darkness. I'd lie awake, struggling to prepare myself for the next day, never sure what questions would come up – and if I'd be able to manage without breaking down in tears.

My mother was not cross-examined on the stand. Her evidence given in Garda interviews was all that was heard during the trial. She portrayed herself as an innocent victim, pressured by Colin into hitting her husband and helping to bring about his death. She informed the Gardaí that on the night my father died she had wanted to take some letters up to Colin and me in the caravan in Corrylanna. I've no memory of letters being brought to us that night. She also said that my father had refused to lend her the car so that she could drive over to us. I found that strange as she could always drive the car whenever she wanted to. She said she'd started walking over to us but that he'd told her she'd 'make a show of him' and decided to come with her. At one point he was alleged to have started walking towards home but doubled back and sneaked up behind her, saying, 'I didn't leave you yet.'

She told the Gardaí that she had been upset when they reached the caravan and had said she wished her husband dead. Then Colin Pinder said, 'I've the very thing to do it,' and produced the silver spanner. She claimed that he had said he would only do it if we all agreed, so we all shook hands on it. In the statement, she said, 'I took that to mean he would kill my husband.' She claimed that I was part of their plan. I did my best to stay composed as I listened to her account, but I felt sick at what I was hearing.

She had told the Gardaí that, on the way home, Pinder had gestured to her three times as a signal that he was going to hit her husband, but she 'had always gestured to him to stop'. She said that when we were back at the house she had climbed through the window to open the front door and heard a thump outside. She described how her husband had regained consciousness and how there had been a chase to the laneway outside the house. In the moonlight, she said, she had seen Pinder raise my father off the ground with a slash hook to the chest.

She claimed she had only hit her husband once and that was because Colin had insisted she do so. It had been later, she said, when he was lying on the ground and she could hear his rattling dying breath. She also described how she'd seen Colin Pinder hitting my father with one of the concrete balustrades that were lying around the garden. I knew the truth – but it was up to the jurors to make up their own minds.

Patrick Gageby put it to Superintendent Aidan Glacken – who had interviewed Vera in 1993 – that she'd been told no prosecution was to be taken against her. When the superintendent said he was not aware of that, he was handed the letter that had been written to her solicitors in 1996: 'I confirm that the Garda investigation into this case has concluded,' he read aloud. The letter had been written by Superintendent Hynes of Granard Garda Station and it went on to say that there would be no prosecution against my mother. I remembered her waving it in my face after it arrived, her confidence returning as my hopes for justice faded. Gageby challenged the idea that the reason it had not been prosecuted in 1996 had been a lack of DNA evidence, citing other cases that had been successfully prosecuted without DNA evidence.

Colin Pinder did not take the stand either. We moved to another courtroom to view a recording of his interrogation in Garda custody. This meant taking the lift. I had stepped inside and the doors were about to close when my mother and her partner entered. We were separated by an abyss none of us would ever be able to cross, yet here we were, crammed into a lift together. It was excruciating. My emotions ran from anger to pity to fury to grief and back again.

The truth was that I hated seeing my mother on trial, witnessing her distress as she listened to the evidence gathering against her. My feelings for Colin Pinder were less confused. He had deserted me, left me alone to bring up our child, and had built another life for himself. Yet it was impossible not to feel some sympathy for him. To the best of my knowledge, apart from the companion I'd seen with him on that first morning, no friends or family members were in court supporting him. My mother had her partner, who would write notes and pass them back and forth to her solicitor, so she had someone to give her advice and encouragement.

I tried to stay calm as I viewed the recording of Colin's statement to the guards. It was a repeat of the story his senior counsel had outlined. Colin claimed that he'd been worried in 1987 about moving to Ireland in case he was subjected to racial discrimination. He claimed that we had not seen my parents for some time after we arrived in Coole – when, in fact, we had actually met my father on our arrival: he had shaken Colin's hand and said he was delighted to see us. He also claimed that my father had refused to allow us to stay on his land and arranged for our caravan to be towed to Corrylanna. Again, I knew differently.

He claimed that my father was working away from home for a few days and my mother told us to stay with her in the house while he was absent. When he returned on the night of his death he'd been drinking and lost his temper when he saw us there. Colin said that a row broke out, with my father becoming argumentative and abusive, taunting him about his colour and yelling at me to 'get out with your nigger boyfriend'.

Aside from the completely false set-up of the night in question, my father was not a heavy drinker; nor had he ever been. He seldom visited our local pub and, at most, he'd take one or two pints. I don't remember ever seeing him drunk. On one occasion when he did go into the Inny Inn, Colin was with him and was introduced to everyone as Brian McGrath's future son-in-law. That was hardly the behaviour of a man who was supposed to be a racist. My father was a well-travelled man who had mixed with every creed and nationality.

Colin Pinder then claimed that he'd attacked my father, who struck his head against the kitchen range as he fell. When he claimed that he had attacked my father for my sake, the pressure in my chest was so intense I genuinely feared I might have a heart attack. During the police interview he stood up and said, 'Will I show you how we did it?' At that point I had to leave the courtroom.

He then claimed that, at a later date, we'd persuaded him to move my father's body and burn it. According to him, my mother said, 'We'll have to get rid of it. We'll have to destroy it. We'll have to burn it.' Whatever discussions around this did or did not take place between himself and her, I was never included in them. As far as they were concerned, I might as well not have existed. They'd leave the room or send me to another room when they wanted to talk privately. I did as I was told, programmed that way from my earliest days. I'd found means of coping, of staying quiet and not asking too many questions.

The jury was told that Colin was crippled with remorse, a depressed epileptic who'd become agoraphobic, and was confined to his flat in Liverpool, tormented by what he'd done. But he based his entire defence on the fact that my father was a racist bigot – and tried to draw me even deeper into the web of lies he had spun to the police. My father could not defend himself against his accusations. He had no barrister in his corner to bring out his true character. Neither could he deny that his death was a tragic accident.

Colin Pinder claimed that after we'd split up he'd often thought of reporting his crime to the police. But then he'd met another woman and made a new life with her.

But the fact that Colin had chosen to leave our son out of his new life, and had made no effort to ease his conscience until he was approached by the police in 1993, raged through my mind as the day drew to a close. I headed off, drained and angry, to catch my evening train and return home to my baby.

The missing piece of the jigsaw throughout that three-year investigation in 1993 was DNA identification. That was the stated reason no prosecution could go ahead – despite the fact that the bones dug up were those of an adult male, and that both my mother and Colin Pinder had admitted their involvement in the crime. As the evidence during the trial unfolded, I finally understood how vital DNA had been in this new investigation – and it was extraordinary, as well as moving, that the half-bucket of charred remains I'd buried in Whitehall Cemetery in 1998 – which were exhumed again in 2008 – had provided the vital key to exposing the truth.

I was particularly interested in a consultant anthropologist who told the court that she had found one human bone at our home in May 2008. Laureen Buckley had examined the exhumed remains with state pathologist Professor Marie Cassidy. About 50 per cent of the skeleton had been recovered, she said, and she'd been able to tell that the bones had come from a male by the pronounced brow ridge. She explained that bone is brownish in colour but turns black when heated by fire. It then turns grey before finally becoming white when completely burnt. The bones she examined varied from unburnt to completely cremated, she said.

The bones were so fragmented that Dr Cassidy could not determine a cause of death. Most had been broken, and Dr Cassidy explained that this could have happened during life or even during exhumation. She said that one half of the lower jaw was unburned and the other half badly burned, showing that it had been fractured before the fire. One of the most horrific and disturbing facts she gave was that my father's right eye socket might have been detached from the rest of the skull prior to burning as one part was fire-damaged and the other was not. At times like this, all I could do was try to shut my mind from the worst of the evidence and pray that the ordeal would soon be over.

The prosecution called Dr Patrick Felle, an anatomist, to give evidence. I'd never heard of an anatomist but I soon discovered that it meant someone with expert knowledge of the human body. It turned out that he'd sifted through a lot of material taken from our land after both digs. He'd found chicken and sheep bones before identifying the human ones.

'The vast amount was fragmented and had been chopped up,' he told the court, and revealed that only the small bones of my dad's right hand and some small foot bones were still intact. Much of the bone was also burned but this hand and part of the jaw bone were not. He had been able to tell only that the person who had died was more than twenty-five years old. The thickness of the bones found 'was consistent with them having belonged to a male of average build', but he could not be certain as so much of the pelvis was missing. Dr Felle said that about a third of my father's vertebrae had been found, with 5 -10 per cent of the total rib mass. There was no sternum, collar bone, shoulder blade or left arm, and only a small percentage of the pelvis had been recovered.

The jury had to look at photographs of the bones as they'd been laid out by the doctor during his examination. They could see for themselves how little of my father's skeleton remained. The information Dr Felle gave was so vivid that I was almost back there, inhaling the suffocating stench that had lingered over our land throughout and after the burning of my father's remains.

My brothers were called to give evidence. They'd been so young then, the eldest barely a teenager. All of them had been mystified by the disappearance of their father. Brian recalled the rows between our parents but no violence – and he'd no memory of what the arguments were about. He remembered Colin taking himself and his two brothers fishing and said he was more like a buddy than an older man.

Andrew spoke about going to England with my mother and brothers, and leaving myself and Colin in Coole. He recalled Colin running to give him a hug on their return home. Each of my brothers had their own innocent memories – and for much of the evidence Colin sat with his head bowed. What was he thinking as he listened to them recalling those carefree days? Did he feel remorse at depriving them of their father? Did my mother have any regret over the lies she'd told her sons, the hurt she'd inflicted on their young lives?

Brian remembered one occasion when my father had beaten him and his brothers. I remembered it also – it was so unusual that it had stayed with me. He had just come out of St Loman's Psychiatric Hospital and must have been feeling particularly humiliated. He didn't want to see or talk to anyone from the community who called to the house. But someone did call and one of the boys opened the door. After the person left my father had rounded on the three of them and, as Brian recounted, had given them a beating.

Dr Patrick Cullen told the court that he'd called to our house three or four times in the 1980s. He remembered the date as 6 March 1985 when my father was committed to St Loman's in Mullingar and identified a hand-written referral letter from that date addressed to the doctor at St Loman's. It acknowledged my father's admission to hospital. He said his decision had been based on my father's past medical history. According to his notes, my father was 'aggressive, agitated and paranoid'. My mother and I seemed 'petrified'. He said the atmosphere in our house when he called was 'agitated' and 'volatile'. If it was, I can honestly say that it wasn't caused by my father's violence – but I would suggest it was because he was terrified of being committed to a mental hospital.

He referred to his notes and said that 'she has bruises on her legs.'

'"They both seemed petrified and daughter has bruises ++,"' said Conor Devally, reading from Dr Cullen's notes. The doctor explained that '++' meant 'lots'.

I don't know about the marks he described. What I

do know is that my father never laid such a violent hand on me. Nor do I believe the bruises Dr Cullen mentioned were inflicted on me by my mother at that time. Surely I would remember a violent beating – just as I remembered the one beating that was mentioned during my brothers' evidence. My mother, who had every reason to blacken my father's name, stated that her life with him had been hard but she did not accuse him of violence against her.

Conor Devally then asked Dr Cullen why there was no mention of him seeing the patient himself.

'My recollection is that Mr McGrath wouldn't wait to be seen,' Dr Cullen replied. He identified an accompanying document, which he agreed had caused my dad's committal to hospital. Dr Cullen had filled in the form in the company of my mother, who had signed a section stating that her husband was not capable of deciding to enter hospital voluntarily. The doctor had signed another section stating that he was of the opinion that my father required mental treatment and was unfit to enter hospital voluntarily.

Conor Devally noted from the letter that my mother and I had complained that my father had delusions and hallucinations, and that he had changed into a violent person, becoming violent over mundane events. Delusions and hallucinations? I was fifteen years of age. I didn't have that kind of language then and, as I said in my cross-examination, why would a doctor take the word of a child in forming a decision to commit someone to a mental hospital? The date of his examination was given as February 1985, but had been crossed out and the word 'Invalid' inserted.

'My understanding of this would have been that I'd actually seen him on the twentieth of February,' said Dr Cullen, although Conor Devally read the date as 10 February. The judge noted that carbon paper seemed to have been used in filling in the form as he could read another patient's address beneath my father's.

Denis Vaughan Buckley questioned Dr Cullen again on his date of examining my dad.

'I may have seen him before,' Dr Cullen said, and explained that he was going by the date that was crossed out on the form.

'Why would you certify someone into a mental hospital who you haven't seen before?' Denis Vaughan Buckley asked.

But the judge refused to allow this question and said he could not cross-examine the witness.

During my own cross-examination I was asked questions about my father's time in Artane. I assume this was to suggest he could have had violent tendencies, having been reared in such a dysfunctional institution. But it was my mother, who came from a normal, affectionate environment, who had lashed out at me over the slightest thing.

Other neighbours took the stand. Michael White, from next door, described one occasion when my parents had visited him and had 'kicked the shins off each other' on their way to his house. He remembered seeing a fire in our garden one evening in late spring or early summer – he could not remember the year but it was after my father had disappeared.

Our local undertaker, Michael Cassidy, also testified to the jury that I'd called into him in 1998 to organise the removal of my father's remains from police custody. Mr Cassidy said that the Gardaí had contacted him ten years later and asked him to point out the grave so that the coffin could be exhumed. Each of the jurors, as well as my mother, Colin Pinder, Justice Edwards and myself, was handed an album of photographs showing the opened coffin with my father's bones inside it.

By mid-July the trial had gone over the estimated three weeks and gave no sign of winding down. Justice Edwards discharged one juror, who had booked a holiday starting that weekend, and the trial continued with eleven. As the afternoons progressed I'd become increasingly stressed over whether or not I'd be on time to catch my train to Mullingar and collect Amy from the friend who was minding her.

There was the constant pressure of seeing my mother and Colin Pinder among the crowd outside, as well as inside the courtroom. One incident that stands out in my mind occurred in the later part of the trial. I was returning to the courtroom one afternoon after lunch when I saw my mother and her partner in the crowd. I also noticed Colin Pinder approaching. We had to wait outside for a few minutes until the door was unlocked. When this happened she moved forward to push it open and, in the same instant, he reached forward to do the same. She looked at him and laughed, her whole face relaxing. For those few seconds she seemed to forget where she was. I wondered how she could step outside the tension and engage with someone who had shared the most hellish of experiences with her. But, then, she had always seemed able to stand outside the horror of that night and not entertain the reality of what had taken place.

Some days were worse than others – but one thing remained constant. The photographers were waiting every time I left the court. I'd been warned by the prosecution team that it would be difficult to deal with the media presence. I was advised to walk past them with my head up and not to cover my face. As soon as I'd appear on the court steps the photographers would start clicking and television cameras rolled. I'd hear shouts of 'Get her! ', 'Run after her!' as they rushed forward from all directions. If I was approaching, they would run backwards, constantly clicking. I did my best to blank it out but I dreaded it. In the evening, when I could bring myself to watch the news, I hardly recognised myself. On one occasion when a group of photographers ran in front of me as I walked towards the courthouse I broke down.

But I adjusted to it. They were doing their job and it was nothing personal. My blank expression hid my fear and embarrassment, the shame I felt I was bringing to my brothers and children as my life was uncovered in such minute detail. All I could do, as Noreen had suggested, was roll with the punches and hope the jury believed me.

Eighteen

The Verdict

The trial finally drew to an end. As I listened to the barristers' closing speeches, I found it hard to believe we were really at this stage. The far-reaching effects of a difficult decision to unburden myself to a friend in a women's refuge in Liverpool were now coming to light. In many ways, it seemed surreal: the wigs and gowns, the formality of the judge and barristers, the curious public, the journalists. And my mother and my ex-husband were seated in the dock, waiting to hear their fate, while I sat on the witness bench, as I'd done throughout the trial.

I listened as Conor Devally and Patrick Gageby challenged my evidence. Conor Devally again suggested that I'd effectively sided with my mother against my father when he was still alive and that I'd helped to have him committed to a psychiatric hospital in 1985. Patrick Gageby told the jury that, in becoming a key witness for the Gardaí, I had played my cards very well. He told the jury that my motivation was that I would be immune from prosecution over my father's murder because anything I'd said while giving my evidence in court could never be used against me.

After making that statement about immunity, the judge ordered the jury and myself to leave the courtroom while they dealt with this legal issue. When we returned, Judge Edwards instructed the jury to disregard what my mother's barrister had said about immunity from prosecution as it was unfounded and incorrect. The truth was that I had never even discussed immunity from prosecution with anybody, and it was not even something of which I was aware could exist. I had never cut any deals, nor were any deals ever offered.

Then it was the turn of the judge to address the jury. Over four days he summed up everything he'd heard during the trial. He told the jury that they were entitled to convict either my mother or Colin Pinder on the basis of joint enterprise. It didn't matter who had struck the fatal blow, if they were satisfied it had been administered within the scope of the participants' agreement. He added that they could not use anything said by one defendant against the other. He spoke of evidence induced on behalf of Colin Pinder 'that might tend to paint her [my mother] in a bad light in terms of sexual mores, honesty and her dealings with authority. You're not concerned with taking a position on any of those things.' He said it was irrelevant whether she had been faithful to her husband, honest, promiscuous, manipulative or deceitful, stating, 'None of that is evidence of propensity to commit homicide.'

Sometimes it was difficult to follow it all but one statement he made cut right into my heart: 'In the view of this court, Veronica McGrath, the chief prosecution witness, must be regarded as having acted as an accessory after the fact, to either the murder or manslaughter of Brian McGrath,' he said. 'The court takes the view that she must be treated as an accomplice.'

He told the jury that, therefore, they should look for corroboration of my testimony. This should be evidence independent of me, should tend to implicate the accused in the offence, and must be credible: 'There are matters in the statements of Vera McGrath Senior capable of corroborating Veronica McGrath's evidence. They'll be a matter for you,' he said. 'I direct you, as a matter of law, that there's no evidence capable of corroborating Veronica McGrath's statement in the case against Mr Pinder.' He added that the jury would not be entitled to find corroboration on circumstantial evidence in this case – and warned that it could be dangerous to convict on the uncorroborated evidence of an accomplice. They could do so if satisfied the witness was both credible and reliable. He said special care must be taken in analysing the reliability of an accomplice.

To me, this was the most devastating statement that had been made throughout the entire trial. I was the chief prosecution witness but, with this pronouncement, I'd become an accomplice. The defence teams for my mother and Colin Pinder had done their best to discredit my evidence. My cross-examination had been nerve-racking and distressing, and it had been equally demoralising to listen to their closing speeches to the jury. I understood that they were defending their clients to the best of their abilities – but I had no one to defend my character. What Justice Edwards had said was more upsetting than anything that had been flung at me by the defence teams throughout the entire trial.

Even since I'd broken my silence in 1993, I'd been coping with people's suspicion, the doubt in their eyes, the gossip, rumours, innuendo. I'd been refused Garda clearance for employment opportunities and had never been given a stated reason why. And now, as the trial drew to a close, the judge had deemed me an accomplice to my father's murder. My head was spinning as I left the courtroom that day. I was furious, yet scared at the same time. Would the jury believe the word of an 'accomplice'? That horrible word kept repeating in my mind.

'What am I supposed to be?' I asked the prosecution

counsel, Denis Vaughan Buckley, when I saw him outside the courtroom. 'Am I a witness or an accomplice?'

He assured me that I was a witness. But the judge had uttered the word 'accomplice' and it was out there now – free for anyone to use. I felt that, in the jury's minds, I could now be viewed in a new and uncertain light.

I left the courthouse humiliated and in tears and faced into the usual barrage of cameras and questions as I headed towards the Luas. I just wanted to get home, collect my young daughter from her minder, and lock the hall door behind me. The full implication of what had been said by the judge really struck home when I was approached by an acquaintance who had been present in court. He suggested that if I was an accomplice, I could use my pregnancy as the reason why I'd taken part in the killing. 'Women can do crazy things when they're pregnant,' he suggested.

I was so angry I could hardly speak. When I got my breath back I told him that I'd nothing to do with my father's murder and had not even been pregnant at the time. But that comment made me aware that I was now in new, uncertain territory.

The next day, the jury was due to deliberate on a verdict for Colin Pinder. I couldn't face the court. I was too upset over the judge's pronouncement, and too exhausted to face the media. If a verdict was reached, they would deliberate on my mother's verdict the following day. I needed to recover my energy for that ordeal. I spent the day at home, trying to catch up on laundry and other chores that had been neglected over the past five weeks. I found comfort in holding my daughter, not having to rush out of the house in the early morning to drop her off with a minder and catch the train to Dublin.

The jury took four hours and five minutes to decide that Colin Pinder was guilty. One of the guards from the cold-case unit rang that evening to tell me they had handed down a verdict of manslaughter. I was shocked that the verdict returned was manslaughter, not murder. Did this mean they believed his version of events – that he'd acted in self-defence when provoked by my father, who'd been portrayed as a drunken, racist bigot? If that was the case, what would they make of my mother's account, which contradicted Pinder's? And did this mean that she might once again walk away a free woman?

On Monday I made the journey to Dublin. Outside the courthouse there was an even larger throng of media than usual. You could feel the tension in the air. I tried to keep my features free from emotion, but inside I felt cold fear. The day passed with agonising slowness. I saw my mother drinking coffee in the café. She appeared calm, but I wondered what feelings her expression masked. She continued drinking her coffee and I walked on. We didn't make eye contact.

Evening came without word of the verdict. A

member of her defence team asked the judge to retire the jury to a hotel for the night, but the foreman insisted that they'd almost reached the end of their deliberations. They didn't want any more coffee or cigarette breaks. As time passed, the judge was again requested to retire the jury for the night – but again this was refused.

As seven o'clock approached and there was still no word, I saw my own stress reflected on the faces of my brothers. By now the jury had been deliberating for five hours. I rang my friend who was minding Amy. She assured me everything was fine with her and wished me luck. Then, just before seven o'clock, one of the guards came out and asked us to return to the courtroom. A verdict was soon to be announced.

One of my brothers decided to stay outside. Each of us had to cope with this very difficult situation in our own way. In 1993, they'd had to deal with the shock and uncertainty of the initial investigation. This trial had left them with an abiding memory of their father's last moments. I wondered how they felt about my part in the revelations. Were they angry with me for going to the police and exposing them to this horror? Or were they angry that I had taken so long to report their father's murder while they'd been fed lies by their mother about his disappearance from their lives? Did they realise how hard I'd found it to protect them from the truth, how terrified I'd been that they'd be taken away from their home – or that I'd be locked away in a mental hospital for making crazy accusations? Sadly, these issues were, and still are, too painful for me to discuss with them.

I could hardly believe that I was the same person as the youngster I'd been all those years ago: eighteen years old and ready to begin my life with Colin Pinder. Yet instead of growing in confidence and maturity I'd gone from one crisis to the next. In the cruellest irony of all, I'd ended up doing to my three eldest children what I'd been afraid would happen to my brothers if I'd told the truth in the beginning: I'd placed them in care.

We entered the courtroom and the court rose for the judge. The foreman of the jury was asked if they'd decided on a verdict. He replied that they had reached agreement and handed the verdict to the clerk of the court, who passed it to Justice Edwards. Then Colin Pinder was brought in by two prison officers through a door to the back of my mother. He was told to remain standing and the judge asked my mother to stand. The jury had reached a verdict by a majority of ten to one. I saw my mother nodding as the judge read out the verdict. Vera McGrath was found guilty of murder.

Hearing those words, I felt a moment of intense relief. My living nightmare was finally over. I'd been freed from fear, from dependence, from the secret knowledge I'd carried for so long. My word had been accepted. The jury had believed me. Even the knowledge that I'd been called an accomplice by the judge didn't seem to matter in that instant.

But as the judge handed down the mandatory life sentence to my mother, a member of the cold-case team sat in beside me and whispered in my ear. I strained to hear the judge, but the detective insisted that I listen and signalled for me to go outside the courtroom. I then heard what I hadn't been able to make out inside. As I'd been declared an accomplice by Justice Edwards, it was possible that I, too, might receive a call from the cold-case team or the local guards in the future.

The feeling of liberation I had experienced only moments before was shattered. Could this be true? And as for what was happening inside the courtroom, the moment was now lost. I would have to read the newspaper reports to find out how my mother had reacted to the verdict. Her partner had cried when the mandatory life sentence was declared, and I believe they had a few minutes to hold each other before she was led away. Colin Pinder would await sentencing until 1 November 2010.

A large group of journalists was waiting outside. My brothers left together and ran the gauntlet of the media – but I felt as though all my defences had crumbled. I knew I wouldn't be able to hold myself together. As the journalists and the public left the court, I sheltered out of sight in the smoking area. I rang a journalist who had been kind to me during the trial. He'd offered to help out with a lift if I ever felt I couldn't manage on my own. He advised me to stay inside until he had driven across the city to collect me.

I'd recovered some composure by the time we eventually left the courthouse. The photographers were still waiting, and ran down the road in front of me. As I tried to keep my head down and ignore them, the main thing I felt was numbness. The enormity of what had happened had yet to hit me. My mother was in jail – and I had placed her there. Yet I experienced no pleasure or satisfaction from that. It was as if all my emotions had been used up.

By the time I had collected Amy and driven home to Coole, the media had arrived there. Their cars were parked everywhere along the road. Journalists and photographers stood around, waiting to interview me. I made my way through them and into the house. By now the numbness had worn off. The loneliness that I'd tried to keep at arm's length since the trial had swept over me – and the words that the cold-case guard had spoken outside the courtroom were fully sinking in.

Next morning I saw the notes journalists had pushed through the door, seeking interviews. Some photographers broke down the fence dividing our garden from a neighbouring property. It was painful to watch them running through the field, trying to find that long-ago shallow grave. I'd never marked the spot. It was obscene even to think of doing so.

I hoped the fuss would die down over a few days

but, until that time, I was afraid to leave the house. When I finally did, to bring my daughter to the crèche, a friend phoned the following day to tell me I'd been photographed outside it by one of the tabloids. My child's privacy had been invaded, and I was disturbed by this intrusion. Every time I went out I imagined photographers lying in wait. Entering a newsagent's was an ordeal as I never knew what kind of lurid headline would be splashed across the front of a paper.

As autumn approached, life took on some semblance of normality. My brothers and I were anxious to have my father's remains buried again in consecrated ground. The weeks passed and we received no word from the guards as to when they would be released back to us. I wondered if we would have a repeat of the difficulties I'd had more than a decade previously when the first investigation was under way. I called one of the officers in the cold-case unit, who told me he would try to hurry the process along.

In early September a guard called to the house and said they were ready to release the remains. At my father's first funeral, his bones had been lovingly placed in a velvet bag and I'd had an opportunity to place some personal possessions beside him before his coffin was closed. This time, we were informed by the guards that his remains would be returned to us in a closed coffin. If we wanted to put any prayers, pictures or anything personal in beside him we had to drop them into the morgue in Dublin before the coffin and hearse left for Westmeath.

The mass was deeply moving and this time, as a family, we felt a sense of togetherness. Sandra, who works in the medical centre in Coole and is a great support to me, is a beautiful singer. She sang during the mass and was movingly accompanied by her son on the violin. I brought red roses, which we threw on to the coffin after it was lowered into our father's final resting place. It was a sad day, yet it brought its own calm. Dad's remains would never be disturbed again. Brian McGrath could finally rest in peace, knowing that justice had been done. I was glad that we were there together, as a family, to say our goodbyes.

Colin Pinder was due to be sentenced on 1 November 2010. For my brothers and myself, the day would provide us with an opportunity to read our victim-impact statements. I had worked hard at putting mine together. When I arrived at the court I gave the statement to a member of the cold-case team, who agreed to read it out for me. Noreen from the court services made sure I had copies to spare in case they were requested. Unfortunately, though, the hearing was cancelled until 29 November.

I planned to drive up on that date with one of my brothers. Heavy snow had fallen during the previous days, and the roads around Coole were heavily banked with drifts. Driving was impossible, even if I'd been able to get my car out of the driveway. The house in

Coole is old, with no insulation in the walls or lagging on the pipes. They'd frozen during the cold snap and the ones leading to the range were in danger of implosion if I tried to light it. I lit a coal fire and stayed beside it for the day as I awaited news from the court. I watched the snow floating down while Amy played around me. We seemed to be the only people alive in a white world, yet beyond the snow, events were unfolding in the Central Criminal Court. In my imagination I was there. That evening one of my brothers texted to say that the sentencing of Colin Pinder had been further postponed until 15 December. However, my brothers' victim-impact statement had been read to the court by Detective Inspector Martin Cadden. This is what the court heard.

> *The loss of our father has had a profound effect on us. Learning of the barbaric way his life was taken away from us has left us numb with shock. Not being able to visit or tend to a Christian burial site has left us with the inability to grieve or mourn in the normal natural way. The loss of our father, and not having a father figure, has left us with no direction in life as children and young men.*
>
> *Our father was a kind, pleasant, hard-working, intelligent, loving man. He is greatly missed by his children and grandchildren, who were denied knowing the wisdom that comes from a loving grandfather.*

The passing of time has not dimmed the
memory of, or longing for, a much-loved father.

I was anxious to know how mine had been received and how Colin Pinder had reacted, if at all. But I was told that his legal team had objected to my statement being read out in court – and questioned how I could be called an accomplice on one hand and a victim on the other. The judge upheld this objection. This revelation was a real body blow. Everything I had wanted to express in court about my father and his untimely death was contained in that statement. I'd tried to say it on the witness stand but had had to cope with constant interruptions from the defence counsels. Now my words would never be heard. I cried myself to sleep that night.

I rang one of the investigating officers to ask about it. He said that as I'd been called an accomplice by Justice Edwards, Colin Pinder's defence team would use that fact to try to achieve a leaner sentence for him. This excuse only added to my distress – and increased the fear I felt over the warning issued by the member of the cold-case team when my mother was being sentenced.

On 15 December Colin Pinder's sentence was finally handed down. I did not attend but read the reports afterwards. Justice Edwards described the killing of my father by Colin Pinder and my mother as 'callous and vicious'. He also described as 'savage, depraved and barbaric' the manner in which his body was desecrated after the killing.

'You were significantly active in the callous disposal of the body,' he said, and refused to accept Colin's arguments that he was under the duress of myself and my mother. 'The manner in which he was killed was extraordinarily vicious. He was bludgeoned to death,' the judge said. 'You weren't the primary participant – Mrs McGrath rendered most of the blows – but when he fell you threw a concrete mould at his head.

'The fact you were involved in such a way weighed heavily upon you. You have realised the horror of what you were involved in and it has caused you suffering,' he added. 'The fact it occurred belatedly is unfortunate. It should not have taken you as long as it did to come forward.'

But Colin Pinder had not come forward, not of his own volition anyway.

The judge sentenced him to nine years' imprisonment, backdated to when Pinder first entered custody the previous July.

There are different kinds of prisons – and different kinds of freedom. Vera McGrath might have felt she was gaining freedom of a kind when she murdered the husband she despised. In doing so, she imprisoned me in a cell of depression, fear and constant anxiety. Now, all I want to do is move on, in the knowledge that, in time, I did the right thing by my father's memory. I want to accept a job without worrying whether or not I'll get Garda clearance but, since the trial ended, I've no idea where I stand regarding the law. 'Accomplice': that one word has changed everything. I don't know if a knock will come to my door one day and I'll be told by a guard that the DPP has made a decision – and that I will stand trial as an accomplice.

I witnessed a murder. Evil unfolded before my eyes and I could do nothing to prevent it. People will always find it difficult to understand why I didn't go to the Garda immediately and report it. In giving this account, I've tried to answer that question properly. Although it has been painful at times, I've written truthfully about my life, warts and all.

My biggest regret is that my three eldest children have suffered because of my difficulties. Throughout my darkest days, I never stopped loving them. But I wasn't always capable of managing the chaotic life they had been born into. I've examined my failed relationships with men. Although some of my children have different fathers, I haven't had many relationships. I had four serious ones over those twenty-three years, and two of those men were my husbands. I involved myself in relationships with men whom I thought could protect me, instead of standing on my own feet. Dependence is a difficult habit to break, especially when the pattern has been set from the earliest days. But now, for the first time, I'm learning to stand on my own two feet. And I'm getting better at it all the time.

I had a bond with my mother. I wish it had been created from love and not from the side-effects of an abusive childhood and, later, those of a heinous crime. That bond is no more. I don't visit her in prison, and we have no contact by letter or phone. I can only guess at how she feels about me. All I know is that it's better this way.

Through the years, why did I keep going back to her? Listening to the evidence in the trial and reading the media reports, you would be forgiven for thinking that I seldom left her side. Yet many years could pass without my returning to her. I've struggled through enormous hardships in my personal life, and it was only ever when I was at breaking point that I came back to her, knowing that, even if she received me coldly, she would understand my reasons for coming home. Many times I believed my life had moved on and I was freed from her dominance. But the events of the past never went away. They were always there, shadowing us. Even Colin Pinder buckled under their impact, becoming solitary and depressed, afraid to go out into the open spaces he'd once loved.

Shortly before my father died he told me he was proud of me. I've never forgotten that. The following words are my testimony to him, to honour his cherished memory, in the form of the victim-impact statement that was not allowed to be delivered in court that day:

It is very hard to put into words how I feel today. It has taken twenty-three long years and a lot of heartache and loss to get to this point. Looking back on my life since the day I lost my father, I can honestly say that the only good memories I have of my childhood are thanks to my dad. He was the rock that kept us all together as a family. He provided the love and affection and put the food on our table. He tried to give us the best life he could afford to give. He was a very hard-working man. After a long day working for a wage he would come home and start working on rebuilding or decorating our home.

He had great principles, despite some of the things that have been said about him in court. It was stated that my father was often drunk, yet I very rarely saw my father take an alcoholic drink. It was also stated that he was a racist and this is something that I want to clear up for once and for all. My father was not and never could be called racist. Over his life he mixed with people of every creed and nationality and he never judged. He had many friends in England of different races and that is why I knew that he would not have a problem with me marrying a man of mixed race, because he was a man who accepted people for what they were, not what they looked like.

As a child and a teenager I always remembered how my father liked to help people who had less

237

than us when he could afford to because he used to say that he remembered what it was like when he had nothing.

His family was his life. He loved my mother and he even told me this on the day he was murdered. She was everything to him and all he wanted was a family, something he had never had himself.

I lived in fear for years of telling what happened outside our home that night in 1987. As a direct result of that fear, and due to the heartache that followed throughout the rest of my life, my own children's lives were devastated and turned upside down.

The events of that night have haunted me for years and still continue to do so. I lost three of my own children to foster care because my whole world fell apart trying to protect my mother out of fear and yet praying that one day I would be able to get justice for my father. I hope that today my father is finally at peace. It will be very difficult for us, as it has been all along, but I hope that we can now try and move on as best we can. Unfortunately, though, the events of that night will always be with us until the day we die.

It has been a long, hard few years but I want to thank the Gardaí and support services for their help throughout the trial and in the years leading up to it. And I hope that my brothers and myself can now eventually move on with our lives.

Not only did I lose my father that day, I also lost my mother, and our whole family unit was shattered. I would ask that the media kindly respect the need for us as a family to have privacy at this time.

Rest in peace, Da.

239

Epilogue

As I write this, I am reunited with my two sons. They are men now, intent on leading their own lives, but we've talked a lot about what happened and why I had to hand them over to the care of other families. Even if they still question my motives in their own minds, I hope they believe that it was one of the most heartbreaking decisions I ever made. The evidence that came out in the trial, however difficult it was to hear, may have answered questions they were afraid to ask in case it upset me. But they know today that I love them with all my heart and I'll be there for them no matter what happens in their lives. Like my brothers, they've had to endure the media attention and the horror of having our family life exposed in court. They never knew their fathers and, for Liam, the exposure of the trial was particularly harrowing. Thankfully, my second son has some contact now with his father and I'm pleased about that.

My daughter, Clare, a teenager now, never knew her father and will only have the earliest memories of me. But we did share those first few precious years. I have always loved her so much. I only walked away to save her from my own desperate circumstances and the distress my depression could inflict on her young life. Leaving her in the care of Social Services was one of the most heart-wrenching decisions I've ever had to make. I am very grateful to the foster parents who have taken care of her all these years.

Two of my daughters are in England with their father and I hope to visit them soon. I talk to their little sister about them every day and show her their photographs. I am determined that they will be part of my life again. My dearest wish for the future is one day to sit at a table with all of my six children to celebrate a family meal. That would be the best gift of all and I live with that hope.

The house in Coole needs constant attention. It's badly in need of repair but, step by step, I'm determined to get it back to the condition it was in when my father was alive. I know how much he loved his house and how much work he did to make it a home for his family. I like to think that he is here, around me, watching over me and his sons.

The nightmares still come, but they're less frequent

these days. I'm often asked if it feels odd or scary living on the land where my father was killed. But I don't find it so, not nowadays. Years ago it was different. Then I did feel fear, as if his ghost was reproaching me. Now I feel that it can rest in peace, and because of that, I can be at peace too.

The past has left its mark on us as a family. We all have our own stories, our own memories, our own emotions about the tragedy that befell us.

Nothing can bring back my father – nor will his memory ever be erased. And I'd like to believe that his memory can make us stronger as a family.

On 27 April 2011, just as this book was going to print, my father's inquest finally took place some twenty-four years after his death. The death was recorded in Mullingar District Court as the result of 'unlawful killing'. It finally brought to a close years of immense heartache and pain for the whole family. I pray that we can now find peace, knowing that he is finally at rest in consecrated ground, never to be disturbed again.

Acknowledgements

Firstly I want to thank Hachette Books Ireland for agreeing to publish this book so that I could finally tell the true story of what happened on the night my father was murdered, and how the events of that night changed my whole life forever.

I want to mention my brothers, all three of them, whom I love more than they will ever know. I want them to know that I did what I felt I had to do, went along with the mad plan that my mother and Colin Pinder drew up, just because I wanted to protect them and because I was terrified of what would happen to them and to me if my mother knew I had gone to the police.

I want readers to understand that I have had to change the names of my brothers and children to protect them from any further intrusion into their lives and I also chose to change the names of my children's fathers and people who were close to us in our lives. These names and some place names have been changed for privacy reasons.

Throughout all of this investigation, right from the day the Gardaí were first informed of my dad's murder, now-retired Gardaí Kevin Tunney and John Maunsell have been there for me at the other end of a phone day or night to advise and support me and I will never be able to thank them enough for their ongoing help and encouragement.

Both Kevin and John believed my story from day one, even though it took many years to eventually get justice for my dad.

They are still there for me today and that means a lot to me. If John Maunsell had not persevered to get my father's remains dug up for vital DNA tests, even after his retirement, I would never be where I am today and I will always be grateful for his faith in me.

I also want to mention the Garda Cold Case Unit, especially Garda Maurice Downey, for finally helping me to get justice for my dad.

Thanks to the Gaffney family in Coole who looked after my baby during the trial. I also want to thank you all for always giving me a smile or a kind word when I knew most other people were gossiping about me behind my back. Your support meant so much to me, more than you could ever imagine, and I will always remember that.

Also a word of thanks to the girls in the Kidz Aloud crèche, especially Siobhan, Annette (Tinette) and Kathleen for their smiles every day and for always giving a little extra attention to my little girl, knowing how hard it has been for us all.

A big thank you to Dr Roy Shuttleworth, a psychologist in London. If it was not for Dr

Shuttleworth I know I would be dead today. He kept me strong when I was at my lowest ebbs.

And to the foster parents who looked after my boys and my daughter when I was very sick and unable to care for them. I am extremely grateful for all your help in raising my children. No mother wants to leave their children to grow up without them but sometimes we have no choice and foster parents do not get the credit they deserve for their help during these times. I want to especially thank the family who took my daughter in and who still care for her today.

I want to give thanks to a fantastic, caring, social worker from Castlerea, Jonathan Weavers, who was a great support to me when I was fighting to have my father's remains buried in consecrated ground. Also Denis Naughten, who was a politician at the time and was the only politician who actually helped me to have my father's remains released. Denis even went as far as to mention the issue in the Dáil at a time when other local politicians ignored my pleas for help and I will be eternally grateful to him for his help at that time.

Although my granny and grandfather have passed away, I want to mention them in this book, because most of my good childhood memories come from my times with my mother's parents and my aunties. Our meetings were very rare over the years but I want them to know that I will always remember each of them with love.

To the Sapphire Unit, part of the UK police force. I

want to thank you all for your help and your understanding when times were especially rough for me and to UK solicitor Anna Gowen who was a sweetheart to me and was there when I needed her most.

And a thank you to the staff in Bellinter House near Navan who, while writing this book, kept us supplied with homemade scones and coffee.

To the memory of my father's pal Louis O'Neill, who has sadly passed away. Louis was such a huge support and friend to my dad over the years and I want his family to know how much he meant to my dad, along with all the men in Coolure House who were there for us over the years.

To the undertaker Michael Cassidy. He was there for both of my father's funerals and he went beyond the call of duty both times to make sure my father had a dignified burial, despite the circumstances.

And to Dr Noel Cogan in Castlepollard and the receptionists Angela and Sandra. I am grateful to Sandra for singing at my father's funeral and to her son who accompanied her on the violin.

I would also like to sincerely acknowledge Garda Sergeant Niall McKiernan in Castlepollard. He has been a fantastic help to me over the years and goes beyond his role with his work in the community.

And to Noreen in Court Support Services in Dublin. This woman I could never thank enough. She was absolutely fantastic when I struggled each day to get through the trial.

I also want to thank Yvonne Kinsella for writing my story. Talking through my life with Yvonne, for all the months prior to publishing this book, has been like on-going counselling for me and she will never know how much she has helped me to pick myself up and finally realise that I am not such a bad person after all.

She has encouraged me to gain some self-confidence and to love myself for a change and I am truly grateful to her for all her words of encouragement.

I also want to thank my agents Prizeman & Kinsella for working with me to get my story published so that people can finally hear the truth. I'd also like to thank June Considine for her help in writing my story.

And last but not least for all of my children. I love you all very, very much and I hope that one day you will all understand why, at times, I had to do things that I didn't want to do.

I am sure there will be many questions in all of your heads as to why your mammy left you in care, or with other family members, on and off throughout your childhood, but please know that what I did I had to do for your own sakes as much as mine.

I was very, very sick and my family home was no place to rear children. I didn't have my own life, I just existed. It was a house filled with lies and deceit and my mind was torn apart as I struggled to get by each and every day.

Please forgive me for doing what I had to do but

always know that I never, ever, stopped loving you all and I hope that one day we can all be together as one big family and finally leave the past and all its horrible memories far behind us.

Love you always.